THE CODE

How to Unlock Your Inner Genius for a Life of Equanimity

Felora Ziari

CRIMSON WOMAN PUBLISHING

REVIEWS

Many of us feel that we deserve more out of life—that we have talents that aren't being utilized. The CODE, by Felora Ziari, takes us on a journey through various levels of consciousness to uncover our deepest desires by stripping away the constraining masks that we adopted to conform to the limiting expectations imposed on us. By giving us a practical roadmap to our goals, The CODE is a valuable augmentation to the concept known as the Law of Attraction. The CODE leads us through a powerful process in which we uncover our innermost desires that can provide the volition to achieve our highest potential.

Ron Frazer, Ph.D.
author of *Staying Well: a family guide to wellness*

Felora believes that we all have a wealth of untouched potential that we have not tapped into. The CODE is a waterfall of wisdom, insight and practical perspectives to help us examine the unexamined aspects of ourselves in order to recognize our unique inner powers and realize our highest potential. She skillfully describes the methods that will enable us to unlock our inner genius and create harmony between our desires, goals and destiny. I highly recommend this book to anyone who is looking to achieve greater success.

Sarah Bird, award winning author
Daughter of a Daughter of a Queen
coming in Fall 2018 from St. Martin's Press

The Code is for anyone seeking to identify and achieve their deepest desires (those that will lead to self-actualization). Felora Ziari offers a practical framework that draws on personal stories of connection and purpose as well as insights from science, religion, and literature to guide readers in shifting mindsets and changing habits to cultivate a sense of gratitude and abundance. This is an important book for anyone seeking to align their thoughts and actions with their true purpose.

Deirdre Mendez, Ph.D.
author of *The Culture Solution*

The CODE: How to Unlock Your Inner Genius for a life of Equanimity

by Felora Ziari

First Edition

Copyright © 2018 Crimson Woman Publishing

ISBN: 978-0-9906974-4-2

All rights reserved. This book or any portion thereof may not be reproduced or used in any manner whatsoever without the express written permission of the publisher except for the use of brief quotations in a book review.

For additional copies, see www.felora.net, www.amazon.com, or your local bookseller.

DEDICATION

In life, you don't choose those who are born through you, but you can choose what is born in you because of them!

To my beloved children Arash and Nakisa, my love for you shall live forever!

You inspired me to embrace the beauty of love in everything I do, and more importantly to serve Love for the sake of Love!

Table of Contents

Dedication
Acknowledgements
Introduction..1
What Is CODE?..5
   Embracing Disorder...6

Unit 1, The Essence of CODE.................13
Butterfly Effect..15
Chapter 1, Higher Purpose.........................17
   Your Heart-Centered Purpose..................17
   My Transformation:
   Seeing The End In The Beginning.......................19
Chapter 2,
The Wisdom of Transformation.................25
   The Power of Thought..25
   What are the Questions We Need to Ask
   Ourselves?...27
   The Power of Self..31
   The Book of Your Life..33

Unit 2,
The Foundation of Self Discovery........37
   Chapter 3, The Process of Self-Discovery.39
      Is Self-Discovery a Linear Process?....................39
      Transforming Anxiety
      into Security and Trust..42
   Chapter 4, Intrinsic Aspect of Self.............47
      The Essence..47
      Meaning of Wisdom...48
      Humility..50

Chapter 5, Extrinsic Aspects of Self..........53
   Shadow Ego..53
   Self-sabotage..54
   What Do I Need?..57
Chapter 6,
Prerequisites for Self-Mastery..................59
   Energy Integration vs. Energy Drains...............59
   Our Programming & Our Choices....................63
   Healthy Boundaries......................................65
   How Does Transformation Happen?...............68

Unit 3, Cultivate..................................71
Chapter 7, Self-Mastery............................73
   What are the attributes of Self-Mastery?..........73
   A path in the woods.....................................75
   Who Owns Our Life?......................................76
Chapter 8, Looking Beyond the Illusion...79
   Living at the Resonant Frequency....................79
   How Do We Interpret Our Reality?...................81
   Our Masks as Programmed Conformity..........86
   Removing Our Masks....................................88
   Mindset Shift..93
   Understanding Triggers................................94
Chapter 9, Six Types of Desire.................101
   Understanding Desires.................................101
   Six Types of Desire......................................103
   The First Desire: Autonomy...............................105
   The Second Desire: Validation..........................110
   The Third Desire: Romance..............................115
   The Fourth Desire: Significance.........................118
   The Fifth Desire: Expression.............................122
   The Sixth Desire: Joy....................................125
   The Flame..129

Unit 4, Observe.................................131
Chapter 10,
Listening to our needs and desires.........133
- Inner Guidance.......................................133
- Are Convenient Choices Holding you Back?..135
- Curiosity Mindset...................................137
- Live Fully, See Fully, Feel Fully.........139

Chapter 11,
Two Pillars of Trust and Detachment.....143
- Pillar of Trust..143
- Trust and Doubt.....................................148
- Pillar of Detachment.............................150

Chapter 12,
Listening to Inner Knowing.......................153
- Emotions are Mirrors.............................155
- The Road We Journey............................163

Unit 5, Develop.................................165
Chapter 13, Optimism.................................167
- Are Your Dreams Big Enough?..............169
- The Power of Gratitude.........................172
- State of Awe..174

Chapter 14, Purging the Clutter...............177
- What Defines Us?..................................177
- Redefining Ourselves............................178
- Let's be True to ourselves....................179
- Determining Your Platform...................181

Chapter 15,
Replacing Barriers
and Self-limiting Beliefs............................183
- Replace Complaining with Gratitude...............184

Chapter 16, State of Grace........................187
   Are We Attracted to Our Desires?.....................187
   Is This Real, or Just a Movie?........................189
   Walking a spiritual path................................190
   Maintaining a Clear Vision............................192
   Setting Boundaries......................................192
   Visualize the Successful You.........................195

Chapter 17, Gaining clarity.....................197
   Beyond Illusions..199
   Are You Looking for the Tracks of the Lion?.201
   Cup of Insight...205

Unit 6, Execute...................................207

Chapter 18, Transformation....................209
   Breakthroughs..209
   Conscious Language....................................213
   Conscious Intention....................................215

Chapter 19, The Birth of a New Life........219
   What am I looking forward to?......................219
   Purposeful Commitment..............................221
   Commitment Exercise.................................224
   Success habits...224

Chapter 20, Alignment...........................227
   Intention of a Successful Restaurateur...........227
   Imagining New Possibilities..........................229
   Visualization Practice..................................232
   From Awareness to Execution......................233
   Remember to Remember............................241

Unit 7, The Gift of Code......................243

Chapter 21,
Becoming an Inner Explorer...................245

About the Author...............................250

ACKNOWLEDGEMENTS

I would like to express my immense gratitude to the many people who supported me in writing this book.

I would like to thank my friend Mandy Cavanaugh for her contribution to this book. Our numerous conversations and her insightful wisdom helped me find clarity around the topics presented in this book.

I would like to thank my friends Joyce Beck, Aniela Costello, and Sarah Jabeen, for their support, encouragements, and wisdom. My deepest gratitude to each of you for helping me reflect on various aspects of self-mastery.

My deepest gratitude goes to my friend Ron Frazer who has not only been an amazing editor but a source of great reflection and inspiration. Thank you Ron for being on this journey with me!

A drop of water contains the secret of an ocean!
The leaf of a tree possesses the beauty of the forest!
A human heart holds the knowledge of the universe.

INTRODUCTION

To understand the truth, knowledge is essential. However, knowledge is meaningless unless it finds expression in our actions and habits. We can never grasp, much less achieve our highest aspirations when our heart is sealed, our mind clouded, or our eyes closed!

Life is a work in progress. Even though this is such a cliché, the truth is we are continuously moving towards some kind of target, defining and redefining our "TO BE" list or our "TO BE" self. Our utmost desire is to unveil and reveal our fullest potential, thus creating the opportunity to thrive! We all want the opportunity to integrate our experiences, our knowledge, our wisdom, our culture, and our beliefs into a creative force that could be the seed for change and transformation! Most importantly we all want to be content, happy, and joyful without having any form of inner resistance to our choices. Without inner resistance, we live lives of equanimity, where insight, reflection, observation, and action help us maintain balance of mind and heart.

What we don't understand, we fear!
What we fear, we avoid!

Although we know that making decisions based on fear affects our progress, most of us are guilty of ignorance, not knowing how to eliminate fear or move forward despite our fear. The very first step in overcoming fear is to locate its source.

The word "unlock" in the title of the book has many connotations. The key that unlocks anything, especially our desires, is a metaphorical representation of a deeper understanding of ourselves, leading to a transcendence over our fears and eventually transforming the outcome of our lives. In order to unlock the door of new opportunities, a blind person needs the key of an alternative tool to replace their natural sight. In that same sense, self-awareness can be thought of as the key that "unlocks" the inner sight, opening us to a new world of "Truth". Therefore, we receive more clarity, are able to move beyond our triggers and stories, we find the courage to move past fears and apprehensions of the past, we indeed, gain access to the information that has always been hidden within us and we find all the right answers, alas. The "key" metaphor can also help us understand others better and move past the common menace of making assumptions about people, by coming to the understanding of the fact that their awareness "key" may differ from ours.

One thing is sure: *what brought you to this point was limited by what you knew.*

And to move forward, there's got to be an expansion of what we know, to accommodate the level of progress which we would like to attain. For the expansion of our horizons and the creation of new possibilities to be effective, we need to develop a deeper knowledge about our beliefs and ourselves. No, I do not for one moment claim that this would be easy; for only by forming new habits, shifting our mindsets, and expanding our knowledge base will we have the determination to work through the challenges that will inevitably arise throughout the process of transformation.

Many books have been written to address personal development, so why another and at this time? This book distinguishes itself from others, providing an edge above others in the same class, by offering a holistic approach to different aspects of personal development. This would then guide you to gain awareness of your innermost desires and create a life of non-resistance. The CODE supports your efforts to eliminate distractions, limitations, habits, and fears that have created anxieties and obstructed the awareness of your core desires.

CODE, as a system of transformation, creates clarity and optimization. It is defined by four elements: Cultivate, Observe, Develop, and Execute.

By following the processes in this book, you will peel back the layers of distortion that life has imposed on

THE CODE

you, therefore freeing yourself up so that you can have an authentic and clear vision of your true self in order for your goals to be aligned with your inner purpose. It is indeed exciting to find out that these new goals are achieved with less effort and less drama.

To create alignment, CODE will impart the key of insight about yourself and your desires and will provide practical processes to gear you towards the realization of your life's legacy and the acceptance of what wants to emerge from within you.

*What you choose to concentrate on and cultivate
drives either your success or your failure.
Choose to live a life of Purpose, Trust, and Surrender
and you will never have regrets!*

WHAT IS CODE?

While guiding you to scrutinize your personal and professional transformational journey with more clarity, the different chapters of this book will guide you to Gain a deep awareness of your essence, Listen to your inner knowing, Declutter what you do not need, Detach from vain imaginings, Trust yourself and your choices, Execute your goals through meaningful plans of action. Through all of these processes, what do we aim to achieve?

The ultimate goal is for you to look at your assumptions and challenges and eliminate what doesn't work, to implement new ideas and behaviors so that life flows easily without you having to second guess yourself and for you to be able to handle new challenges more effectively.

CODE as a transformational framework is a reminder that we all need to have a Code to live by that will not only strengthen self-vitality, but also make us benevolent, empathetic and compassionate persons.

The overall theme of each chapter is as follows:

Embracing Disorder

While writing this book, I came to a very important discovery: that there are different aspects to personal transformation that cannot be described in a linear 1-2-3 methodology. I discovered this while trying to create a clear picture of how transformation can unfold in a manner that was simple and easily followed. However, I found that by constraining the transformation to a simple process, I was limiting both the message of the book and my ability to write it. Simply put, it wouldn't be good enough, and the book would lack power if personal transformation were limited to one's obedience to certain rules.

Wouldn't it be immensely delightful for there to be such a linear process that led to the transformation of lives, such that an individual who was once a victim of circumstances changes his or her life into one of self-mastery? Indeed, I would like to be able to give you a step-by-step process. However, while there are steps, I must make it clear that they are not linear. We all have to visit them and revisit them at different times, over and over as we grow in self-mastery. For instance, after reading this book, you may feel that you have a sense of your inner knowing. Hopefully, that has led to some progress in the understanding of your desires. But then, you learn something new or have an experience that brings more clarity and so, you redefine your desires somewhat, and then move on. As time flies by, other opportunities arise and your inner knowing gains even more clarity. It turns out that there really is no end to this cycle of transformation!

There are no straight paths to the destination, of this journey. In order to enable our creativity to reach its fullest potential, we need to embrace disorder as a prelude to order and clarity. Initially, we might be mystified with the different ideas presented to us; but keep in mind that we need to go through some chaos in order to understand the different layers of our personality and to expand our perspectives, to broaden our horizons.

The Code

The block I was facing was the avoidance of disorder, which in reality is a misnomer. I realized something rather astonishing: there is an order within disorder (Highlight). This apparent contradiction is created when we think we perfectly understand what order is. We proceed with that flawed understanding to assume that disorder simply means a lack of order. However that is not the case. As we evolve from one chapter of our lives and into the next, we come face to face with this concept. It is amazing to discover that disorder doesn't prevent our growth and progress; rather it creates the opportunity to look for new or different solutions.

In working through the struggles and challenges of my own life, whenever I was able to "sit" with disorder—or the lack of what I thought order was—until I could "see the end at the beginning," I realized that I achieved more clarity and understanding from this so-called "disorder" in my life.

The four elements of CODE will allow your inner power to exert its will through the alignment of all your senses, creating the "Magical Life" of serenity and inner contentment.

FELORA ZIARI

The Code

CULTIVATE

People who have tapped into the wisdom of desire are curious. They seem to:

- Actively evaluate the basis of their belief
- Understand that in order to know their purpose, they need to understand their true desires
- Cultivate a deeper understanding of the truth of their stories without the need for personal gain
- Understand the causes of discomfort, resistance and anxieties

OBSERVE

People who know the wisdom of their desire experience a sense of flow, in which:

- They are a witness to their own lives and allow life to unfold effortlessly
- They are aligned with their purpose
- They see the "Truth" without judgment
- They accept feedback in order to achieve their highest aspiration or purpose
- There is a feeling that time is slowing down, and that they are in the zone of high performance
- A sense of peace is readily available

DEVELOP

People who are tuned into the specificity of their desire and its wisdom:

- Realize that there are enough resources to achieve their goals
- Practice gratitude, grace, and calm
- Appreciate life in general
- Attract like-minded people into their lives due to their alignment to Self
- They develop optimistic outlook to life, with firm personal boundaries
- They have purity of motive and hence attract more abundance into their lives and careers

EXECUTE

Those who understand the wisdom of their desires:

- Understand that the primary drive of all desires, at its core, is to celebrate and be in a state of joy. This celebration then can become a means, rather than simply the end
- Celebrate what they are grateful for. This will bring more of what they appreciate
- Imagine their outcomes already fulfilled while their intent and the universe line up to that reality
- Create new habits that lead them to greater breakthroughs
- Are in a continual state of Awe and discovery

UNIT 1
THE ESSENCE OF CODE

The Code

BUTTERFLY EFFECT

Ah, the butterfly. That beautiful symbol of transformation is indeed a wonder to behold. Its journey from a caterpillar to a stunning butterfly is a cornerstone of life unfolding through a firm grasp of the existing conditions, overcoming challenges and then surging onwards into the vast space of beauty, grace and inevitable elegance with trust in the universe.

When the butterfly was a caterpillar, it only focused on one thing—what was in front of it—as it crawled around each day. When it naturally enters a dark cocoon, it completely breaks away from what it was; its previous identity with breath-taking conviction. This darkness provides ample opportunity for the caterpillar to change and to emerge into the beautiful butterfly before re-introducing itself to the world. Hence the caterpillar gets to evolve deliberately while being mindful and accepting of the current conditions yet, still trusting the outcome of the future. Soon enough, the regal butterfly emerges, a confident being, flying away with so much trust in the universe to supply its needs.

Pause for a moment and meditate on the butterfly's transformation, of the steps it takes en-route to "becoming." That is you. Your transformation and that of the butterfly are both astonishingly similar. In *Cultivating* ourselves, we go on the journey to "Understanding Who We Are," trusting our journey without any judgment of our present conditions or of what is in front of us. We *Observe* as we enter the dark cocoon of self to shake off what doesn't serve us anymore in order to "Understand Who We Want to Be." We *Develop* "New Mastery" by allowing the space to change, letting go of what we don't need, breaking down the illusions and what needs to be fixed and what we need to develop. We *Execute* by moving forward, letting the light of consciousness enter the dark cocoon, being present to the moment and committed to what is in front of us, and then finally, we fly away regally, with a fresh perspective on our lives. We are struck by the beauty of the process, as effective as it is deep, as strengthening as it is rigorous.

Two factors contribute to a butterfly's successful transformation. The first one is the ability to *Focus on what is in front of it* and the second is to *Trust both the process and the outcome of the transformation.*

CHAPTER 1
HIGHER PURPOSE

Your Heart-Centered Purpose

The intention of this book is to cause a paradigm shift in our minds, reforming our mindsets so that we can open our hearts, pouring immeasurable love into the pursuit of our true desires. With that new mindset, we can plunge head-first into our visions and dreams with both our minds and our hearts.

We all have a Higher Purpose!

Before we can reach our goals, achieve our set objectives, however; we've got to attain mastery over ourselves. We also have an inner knowing of what that purpose is; although limiting messages during childhood and adolescence may have distorted or obscured it. We all have deep desire to manifest our Higher purpose.

Everyone wants to be happy, to do what they love to do, to enjoy what they are doing, to love and be loved, and to gain valuable life skills that make them happy. Embedded in the book you hold, are precepts that would guide you towards an unshakeable recognition of what lights you up, what brings you joy and, most importantly, what enables you to honor your accomplishments and not allow external hindrances to hold you back.

If you are to achieve more while being true to yourself, you must allow growth to take place in an organic, sequential manner; giving yourself enough freedom to question the unspoken agreements that you have made with yourself. Unfortunately, we have been trained to suppress creativity and growth by our culture and upbringing. Instead of creativity and self-expression, we were groomed in uniformity and conformity. You need to break through the limiting messages you have received throughout your life especially in childhood and reveal the sacred nature of your purpose and your nobility. It will allow you to purge that which is not from your Higher Self, and which does not fit with who you truly are in your heart, enabling you to advance into a life of joy, success, and contentment.

In the past, if you are like most of us, you have alienated yourself from your true desires in pursuit of social or creating a financial safety net. You may have wanted to avoid seeming selfish or creating emotional conflict. Being part of a tribe, therefore, meant you had to blend into a group whose beliefs and interpretations may have conflicted with your inner knowing. You may have succumbed to a programming defined by family, mass media, religion, or popular culture. In the process of conforming, you became desensitized to your innate sense of who you truly are. are intended to help you understand your programming and tap into your innate desires and hence upgrade your life.

When you tap into your desires and hear the song of your true calling, you can explore living a life with joy and contentment. You will be in a state of Awe and Wonder where the true majesty of a creative life will be unfolded. The processes outlined in this book are intended to help you understand your programming and tap into your innate desires and hence upgrade your life.

My Transformation: Seeing The End In The Beginning

Transformation can happen in the blink of an eye or through a series of challenges and tests. This story, as I would come to discover later, was a surprise on so many levels. One day, I unexpectedly ran into a childhood friend. As we hugged, a memory flooded my mind in a hurry, as if to prevent me from losing it, bringing back in a rush, a most miraculous event which occurred to me at the tender age of five, an event that would define my life and my perception of life from then on!

While growing up, I loved visiting my father's farm, situated about thirty minutes outside my home town, Shahi, in Iran, where I was born and raised. The farm included livestock, fish, multiple crops and fruit trees. It was a beautiful and serene place with a narrow creek running through it. I especially enjoyed visiting the farm during the rice harvest as then, it bustled with so many activities. My friend's family members were the caretakers of this farm and as such, they lived on the property. She and I enjoyed spending time together whenever I visited.

One day, during the rice harvest, I was playing with my friend in the front yard of her home. My father and his crew were working in the rice paddies. We could hear them from a distance; laughing and singing as they worked. Oh! It was a joyful scene to behold. Little did we know that something terrible was about to happen. While my friend and I were playing, something devastating happened. She accidentally pushed me into a well, which was deep and full of water. She screamed for help, not knowing what to do.

By chance, one of the workers happened to be passing by as he was returning from a storage area, which was close to where we were playing. He witnessed this incident, ran to the well and dropped inside to save me. I remember being pulled under the water and as I resurfaced for the third time, he was able to grab me and rescue me. The others heard the screams and ran to where we were. I was quickly revived. As I grew up, this traumatic incident faded from my memory.

Decades later, as fate would have it, I met that friend again. With a simple hug, those emotions, feelings and the effects of that fall resurfaced in my mind with such clarity. I came to realize that it had an amazing influence upon my life and reflecting on it revealed an even greater impact.

You see, as I was falling, I felt like I was flying, only in slow motion. Surprisingly, I perceived this dark hole to be something magical, waiting for me to experience. I felt no fear, rather a deep knowing that I would be taken care of; "trust" washed over me. As I resurfaced the second time, I took a deep breath and again, was pulled under. That instinctive breath, that gasp, taught me that an innate life force was working in and through me. That one moment—that one chance accident—would forever change my perspective on life. Even as a child of only five years old, I felt completely detached from the outcome. I was experiencing every moment of life as if it was happening in slow motion. I realized at that moment that every breath is a gift. To this day, I have this deeply engraved knowing and belief that I am always taken care of, regardless of the difficulties and challenges before me. For I trust in "Something" beyond my knowing and my imagination.

Within those brief moments when I was fighting for breath in the well, I came to a realization—a certain knowing—of the fact that the invisible air, our breath, connects every human being on Earth. It wasn't intellectual knowledge; it was more of an experiential form of knowledge. Reflecting on that accident as an adult, I realized that our perception of what we see, our definition of fear and the interpretation of events in our lives are usually limited to what we have been taught or experienced. No one knows more than that to which he or she has been exposed. However, there is a magical, *Creative Force* that can easily be tapped into when we understand the unifying connection of our breath to the expansiveness of self-awareness.

Our breath is the most elemental life force—one that everyone in the world shares through inhaling and exhaling the very same air in order to live. Have you ever paused to think about that? We all share the very same air! It is a vast provision which has no form of segregation, it's meant for all of us, to be shared by all of us, and no one is given a larger quota than is given to another person. The knowledge of this common thread creates an awareness that can eliminate the separateness we may feel at times because of how we were raised, influenced and educated.

After I was rescued and recovered, I decided, "To see the end in the beginning," to seek the bigger picture, to discern from the end result, to be liberated from separateness, and not allow my limited perception or experiences to veil my understanding—to be a seeker of Truth and to live a life that was filled with Meaning, Purpose, and Benevolence! I would not rely on the momentum of the wind to be the impetus that would propel me forward. No! I would be guided by the Light at the end of the tunnel. This mindset gave purpose to my existence on earth and served as a compass to move me forward.

The memory of this event lends powerful meaning to my life and has paved the way for my life to unfold effortlessly in the midst of turmoil and uncertainty, allowing me to walk with Grace in the Mercy of the Divine. The well became a symbol of comfort in a space of uncertainty, a reminder to "trust" that there are mysteries beyond my limited perception and understanding of what I know, comprehend or see. *The Well,* through my dear friend, became the instrument by which I came to see Light instead of darkness and feel gratitude for the gift of every precious breath, choosing not to focus on what might be lacking in the moment.

The understanding that every action—every decision—affects everything else in my life has been a gift. I believe that extraordinary things can happen in an ordinary day if we feel the magic of life and cultivate a sense of awe for all that life offers us.

The CODE can liberate what is locked within us when we learn to Trust and become attracted to our inner Light as it moves us towards greater possibilities by consciously choosing to "See the End in the Beginning."

> *The hurt and sadness of the challenges we face in life are inevitable. However, overreaction or prolonged grief makes life more difficult. It inevitably hinders our happiness and our growth. When we have a clear vision of our divine purpose, we are willing to accept the hurt and sadness that we encounter in our journey to our goal. Each step toward the goal is celebrated, no matter whether that step is uphill or downhill. The greater the clarity of our vision, the greater is the celebration.*

CHAPTER 2
THE WISDOM OF TRANSFORMATION

The Power of Thought

A review of the last several decades shows an accelerating rate of consciousness regarding the role our thoughts play in creating our reality. The field of positive psychology has been teaching us how to achieve more by training our minds. There appears to be a direct relationship between our thoughts and the later events in our lives. Recent physics has shown us that the expectation of an outcome can influence that outcome at the level of particles and waves.

Several factors have brought us to today's unprecedented opportunity in the history of humanity: amazing upgrades in awareness, the expansion of the middle class throughout the world, and the interconnectivity that the Internet brings to us.

Studies have shown that about 40% of our actions are out of habit and are not from conscious thinking. Also, until recently it was thought that we were born with certain characteristics and personality traits that cannot be changed. However, there are many studies in the areas of neuroplasticity (also called brain plasticity) that prove that our brain's neural synapses and pathways are altered by environmental, behavioral, and neural changes. Now we know that our brain can restructure itself irrespective of preset genetic coding, thus learning new habits and behaviors. With this understanding, not only is transformation possible, but amazingly enough, it is in our own hands. For example, a person that was born shy can change the neuronal connections by repeating new habits with different traits and behaviors, thus transforming themselves into an outgoing person.

> *To strive for a meaningful life, we need to look for opportunities that expand our knowledge, wisdom and fortitude.*

We are what we repeatedly do. Excellence, then, is not an act, but a habit. — Aristotle

For transformation to be permanent, it must begin with us striving for something beyond our own personal gratification; successful transformation needs to have as its basis a life lived with significance and impact. To strive for meaningful lives, we need to look for opportunities that expand our knowledge, wisdom and fortitude. This transformative journey starts with the development of the Self, and then spreads outward to our interface with others, and then to the way we show up in the world at large through our actions.

One of the most critical foundational aspects of self-transformation is how dependent it is on having empathy, not only for others but also for ourselves. Our beliefs and our values have a great influence on our transformational process. All of us must maintain a level of belief that is free from the influence of obsolete ideas or mindsets; rather we must find out for ourselves what we stand for and what we value while practicing empathy and compassion.

What are the Questions We Need to Ask Ourselves?

You are the only real obstacle in your path to a fulfilling life. — Les Brown

Who am I? This is a question that almost everyone struggles with. Our lifelong journey of self-discovery and self-mastery leads us to a deep understanding of the core of who we are and who we are meant to be. As the discoveries unfold, and as we understand and—most importantly—learn to celebrate ourselves, we get to sustain lives of contentment. The Nobel Laureate Szymborska said, "Whatever possibility is, it's born from a continuous, 'I don't know'." The journey of life is a progressive movement. It starts with innocence, proceeds with several realizations of "I don't know," and then, when we are on the right track, ends in knowledge, wisdom, joy and surrender. On the other hand, if we are on the wrong track and not moving forward in wisdom and knowledge, we will have more pain, anxiety, inner imbalance and unhappiness. To discover our inner reality, we need to unravel the truth about us and understand ourselves better.

Only with truth we can move forward!

The early chapters of our lives provided our first definition of who we would become in the future. Our childhood story strongly influences our decisions and choices later in life. When we were born, we were innocent and did not know right from wrong. Our world took shape as we grew; we formed opinions, understanding, and knowledge from our environment and the people who were close to us. As soon as we could talk and learn, we began absorbing their opinions and the ways in which they made decisions. By watching the behavior of others, we came to know that light and darkness, good and bad, joy and pain coexist. We lost some part of our childhood innocence, developed our moral values, and then began to understand the limits of our freedom. Our perpetual needs influenced our perceptions of life and our choices. We sought and pursued the things that mostly benefited us.

The discovery of self requires an understanding of the interactions between the three aspects of mind, body and spirit. *If we can let go of the nonessentials,* we will have a better understanding of the mind, body and spirit interaction. When we let go of our attachments to what we have known or learned and the nonessential aspects of our lives, we are able to open up—to discover ourselves in a new way.

However, when we think only about our personal gains, about what would benefit us, or about what others can do for us, we lose sight of the reality of who we are, which eventually will cause resentment, disappointment and unhappiness. While we strive for the recognition that our false mask invokes, we avoid the hard work of acquiring and practicing praiseworthy attributes. For example, we may do anything to make others perceive us as compassionate, kind, or just while simultaneously believing that it is less important to actually be compassionate, kind, loving or just—especially if no one sees our true nature or applauds our attributes.

We have all experienced challenges, tests and encountered difficult ordeals that made a truly lasting impact. These experiences often become defining moments that impact us to the point that we feel like we have lived two separate lives. One's perspective changes so much after such events that we begin to feel like we are putting on different skins, that we are different human beings—in fact, it feels like there is the creation of a "before and after" version of ourselves. People that have had near-death experiences always talk about how their view of life changed from how it used to be. These defining moments may not be as extreme as near-death experiences; they could include a death in the family, a divorce, an illness or an accident. These defining moments influence us tremendously. Some people expand their perspectives on the meaning of life and their purpose, becoming aligned with their higher self, while others shrink to the point of becoming bitter and angry, taking the alternative route of moving towards their lower nature.

When we gain wisdom and perspective from these occurrences, we become kinder, more thoughtful, loving and compassionate. Then these tests and difficulties can be our teacher or our guide, helping us expand who we are so that our actions become aligned with our higher self. For such people, these defining moments are the onset of self-discovery and self-mastery. However, if we allow these circumstances and incidents to hurt our self-confidence or self-esteem, our lives, after the defining moments, might be influenced by fear and apprehension. We might shrink and live our lives in a state of stagnation and struggle. While in such a state, we may be successful in one area of life, but are struggling and out of balance in other areas of life.

As much as we want to avoid chaos, tests and difficulties in our lives, the ultimate truth is that those hard times can be breakthrough experiences for us. They challenge us to look within and find the strength not only to deal with the chaos the best way we can, but also to examine our responses to the crises in order to learn about ourselves. If we handle crises well, we might just have discovered depth and solutions to lifelong struggles throughout our lives.

Every ordeal can be an opportunity for a greater awareness of our true self. How we use the gifts of setbacks sets us apart! These gifts provide potent revelations of our truth and serve as a guiding light that transcends our human conditions.

The Power of Self

Illusions, misunderstandings, lack of knowledge, and negative experiences all create dust on the mirror of self. Therefore we all take on a mixed understanding of who we truly are. Most of our personality and belief system is influenced by our past experiences. While growing up, we create a distorted narrative about our identity, and then we behave in a way that is consistent with this distorted perspective.

There are three aspects to each one of us: the imagined self, the public self and the true self. These three aspects sometimes appear separately and sometimes they mix in various combinations.

The imagined self is who we think we are, based on our interaction with others and our surroundings. We create the imagined self in order to protect ourselves from our environment, to be accepted by parents or friends and to meet other people's expectations. It often becomes a subconscious aspect of our psyche.

The imagined self takes on other people's perception of us. For example, if they perceive us as old, young, fat, kind, mean, beautiful or ugly, then their perception influences us; and as such, they become co-creators of our personality. Alternatively, if we were born blind and were never told that we were beautiful or ugly, tall or short, we would grow up being who we truly are, a human being, without defining ourselves by other people's perceptions of what we look like. The imagined self is not only defined by the reactions of those around us, it is influenced by our culture, our movies, TV, and advertising images.

The imagined self is the combination of the stories of our past, the experiences of the present moment and our future goals. Sadly, with all of these elements in place, our true essence is buried, causing us to forget our true self. Most people are not aware that the imagined self is false; they are led to assume that this is who they really are. It is with the aid of the imagined self that an anorexic, malnourished woman sees herself as fat.

On the other hand, the public self is how we want others to see us. We show our selves differently in different situations, all so that we can maintain a certain image. We are aware, on some level, that the public self is somewhat false. We may present a personality who is serious and studious in a business meeting, but easy going and playful when we are with close friends at home. Of course, we are not trying to be deceptive; and as a matter of fact, different situations require different etiquette and behavior.

To really understand who we are, our "true self," we need to identify the stories of the imagined self, and the shadow aspect of the public self. The best and most valuable gift we can present to ourselves in life is the discovery of the "true self".

> *The meaning of your "true self" is not about being perfect; rather, it means to understand who you truly are, to be comfortable with yourself and then cultivate the best version of you—a unique person who allows their destiny to unfold without resistance.*

The Book of Your Life

The life of each of us is like a unique book that comprises of several chapters, each chapter representing a stage of growth. As we evolve through the life lessons in each chapter, we master those lessons and then we move on to the next one. Each chapter helps us get closer to understanding our purpose—it seems as though we are dancing our own unique dance, following the natural rhythm of our inner music. Hence we gain more clarity about our identity and our expression in the world.

As we complete each chapter of our own book, it feels like leaving the womb of the world we know and then finding ourselves in the noisy chaos of another realm or domain that is unfamiliar. This, we must note: In order to move forward, we need to grasp the lessons of each chapter, gain the spiritual strength and knowledge of that realm so as to make us equipped to thrive in the next phase of our lives. Inherent in each of these chapters is a higher level of capability that enables us to overcome the challenges of the succeeding phase. Along with our new self and our new abilities, we have to learn a new level of personal accountability.

If we fail to attain the capabilities that each phase demands of us, and if we lose the sense of urgency to do so, we may be tempted to delude ourselves with a false sense of self that would retard or block any further progress. In fact, we sometimes need to be left in a particular phase, what we called 'stuck' in that phase for a much longer period, until we are comfortable with our new self and its new capabilities. A major drawback to approaching an understanding of our life's purpose is that we think everyone else has experienced the same life lessons and therefore can understand what we have gone through. It is easy, yet dangerous, to assume that everyone else has the same perspective. In the face of assuming that everyone else has experienced what we have, we expect them to act in a certain way—and it truly baffles us when they don't. 'Why?' we question in rage. Often, this results in resentment, and it prevents us from achieving clarity about our own life journey. By understanding that we are each on a unique journey with different knowledge and perspectives, we can avoid judging others and can then focus on our own progress.

The other challenge is that since most of us are looking to be part of a tribe or a community, we are apt to conform to the behaviors of selected individuals— either to fit in or because we admire them to the point that we lose ourselves in them. Sometimes we want their approval so badly that we abandon our own life to mimic them and follow them on their life's journey. Not too surprisingly, when we follow others blindly, and not for the sake of gaining more knowledge and wisdom, we eventually become resentful since we cannot completely understand their goals and aspirations. Why they would choose to go on a certain route and not on another doesn't make as much sense to us as it does to them. When they choose to go on their own path without giving us any explanation for their decision, it can create a sense of disloyalty in us. However, when we choose to follow the chapters of our own book while gleaning from others and yet dissecting truth for ourselves, we follow a path with a clear roadmap that is aligned with our innate characters, desires and strengths, impelling our lives to flow easier while creating more joy and bliss.

I have seen the power of an ocean, I have seen the majesty of a mountain and the beauty of nature, but I have never seen a more magnificent beauty than a heart that pursues the chapters of their own book and understands the wisdom of their own desires. Nothing is comparable to the joy this person experiences. Nothing.

UNIT 2
THE FOUNDATION OF SELF DISCOVERY

CHAPTER 3
THE PROCESS OF SELF-DISCOVERY

Is Self-Discovery a Linear Process?

Before we can understand the layers of belief about ourselves and delve into CODE, we need to understand certain concepts and theories that can deepen the understanding of our perception, mindset and thought process. We have to understand that this transformation is not linear; we cannot lay out steps 1, 2 and 3 that will work for everyone because each person is unique and their lives are continuously changing. Therefore we might describe this process of self-discovery to be more like a detective novel with many twists and turns, the detective revisiting the clues over and over, and as he does so, a deeper understanding dawns on him. However, unlike a detective novel, the pieces of your life's story don't all fall into place at the end; instead, your life keeps changing throughout the process. Therefore, even when you have accomplished a high degree of self-mastery, the adventure will continue, providing you with more challenges to keep life moving forward.

As will be explained later in this book, everything we encounter around us, including human beings is a system. Each system needs energy in order to function. It also needs to be self-correcting in order to be sustainable and to create the best results in the long run. Our lives self-correct themselves by accessing different aspects of awareness and concepts that are presented in this unit.

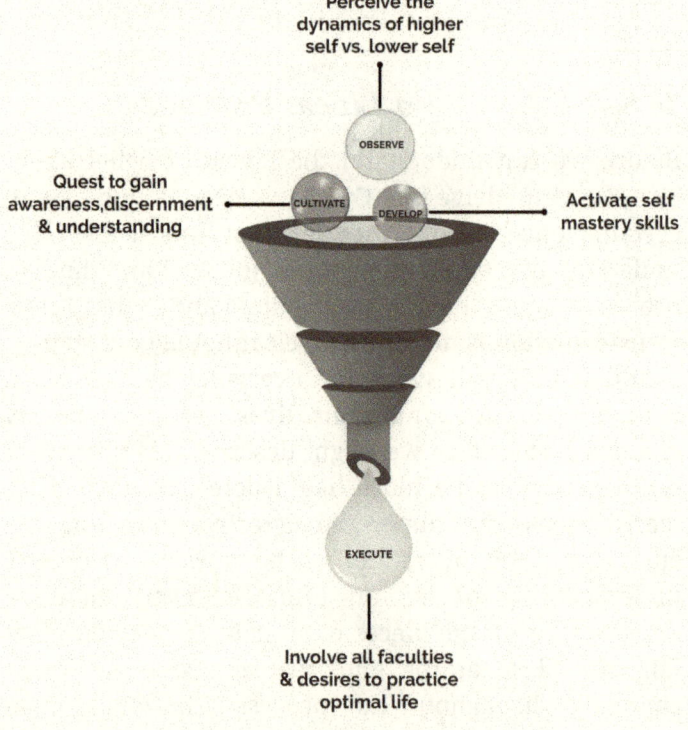

We also need to realize that, in a certain sense, life can be compared to the games that we played as children. Although the objective of those games was to win, we also intended to have fun and enjoy the process. We couldn't anticipate our opponent's moves or know their motives. However, as the game played on, we kept our eyes on what we needed to do to win fairly while enjoying the game. We tried to be the sort of individual who ensured that our opponents were having fun as well. Another aspect of those games we played as a child was the beautiful simplicity which they possessed. Now, what did we do if a game was simply too hard? Well, we simply gave up! If there was no fun involved, our response would be simple: we wouldn't play.

Let us bring these lessons into our current living circumstances:

> *As an adult playing the game of life, if we let fear of the outcome of the game or of our opponent's moves control how we play our game, then we might avoid part of the game, or we might give up too soon. The objective should be to enjoy the process.*

So, let's welcome the randomness that life offers us, embrace the process, have fun and remember:

- Fear creates a need to control the outcome, while joy creates harmony with the outcome!
- A game that is played with the intention of fun for everyone, is a win-win situation!

Transforming Anxiety into Security and Trust

In psychology, there is a term called the false-consensus effect in which people believe, or overestimate, that their opinions and belief are normal and that the majority of people share the same values and belief systems. If we incorrectly perceive that everyone agrees with us, this creates over-confidence, leading to shock, disbelief or drama when we are faced with the reality that others do not share our opinion. If the false-consensus effect continues in us, we might make the assumption that there is something wrong with anyone who disagrees with us. For example, some religious people believe that pious and religious people do not drink alcohol. However, in some cultures, drinking alcohol is very normal and is part of their culture, possibly even part of their religion.

Lack of awareness and understanding of our belief system, and how it compares to the belief system of others, can create biases from a false-consensus—biases that cause division, disharmony and anxiety.

These same biases can prevent us from understanding ourselves better and accepting our shortcomings. At each step of transformation, a major aspect of the process is peeling away layers of cultural programming that have formed masks and obscured our inner knowing. As we fulfill our purpose in life, we must continually be on the alert for obsolete, conflicting or untrue messages from our childhood that have crystallized within us to the point where they now create inner conflict or disharmony. Perhaps we have always held the belief that rich people are always greedy individuals who are only out to cheat others. As we progress toward our goals and find ourselves making more money, there may be a nagging voice telling us to go no further because that would involve cheating people. We may feel that we should not desire more income. These voices that come from our old programming may cause us to ignore our desires. At the very least, they produce anxiety.

Transform your anxiety into security by accepting your inner knowing and indeed, you will begin to understand your calling better. Some people say, "I do not really know my calling" or "I cannot clearly hear my inner knowing." The reason for this lack of clarity is because we are not truly living our own authentic lives; rather, we have chosen to water the lives of others, to accept without questioning, the perceptions and opinions that others have about us, perceptions that are in fact, limited to who they are and what they want to achieve in life—all of which may be different from what we perceive or want.

You might ask, "How can I live an authentic life until I know my calling?" A good question! The answer is this:

> *This process is a cycle; we start with some limited understanding, develop some goals, act on them, get more understanding, revise our goals, and the process continues. The point is, you have to start where you are, with the understanding you have today. You cannot wait for absolute clarity; you get absolute clarity by acting on an understanding that is less clear, and then revising your goals as time goes on.*

It could be that you are so busy living your life that you are not listening, or tuning into what you really want. Pause and take a deep breath. You need to be perceptive in order to recognize the invitation of your higher self. Women are often juggling children, jobs, husbands, and volunteer responsibilities—like a juggler spinning plates atop a dozen poles. You may feel that there is no time for introspection or self-development activities. If you take a little time each day for introspection, you will find that you are a better mother, wife or coworker.

> *You really owe it to yourself, your family and your community to do the work necessary to uncover your inner knowing and define your desires.*

This process helps you learn to love, respect and especially honor every aspect of life that serves you while identifying and clearing out the things that do not. Everyone has light and shadow aspects. At every intersection of life, you need to be present to life and summon the Light to lead you so you can arise to your noble self. Ram Dass, a great spiritual leader said, "We need to learn about the world, and then empty it." The world has so many layers, layers that are meant to be peeled back, to be unraveled. When you empty the physical world, you are able to understand the other dimensions of the world that are spiritual. As much as you may want to gain knowledge, at times you need to purge your knowledge so you can see with a new set of eyes and gain new understanding.

Remember that life is like a game and the purpose of the game is not only to win but also to have fun and enjoy every aspect of it.

The difference between great people and everyone else is that great people create their lives actively, while everyone else is created by their lives, passively waiting to see where life takes them next.

The difference between the two is the difference between living fully and just existing. — Michael E. Gerber

The Code

CHAPTER 4
INTRINSIC ASPECT OF SELF

The Essence

Human nature is essentially good and pure. We have been created in the image of God, the image of Love and Goodness. When we are born, we do not know the concept of good or bad. Our basic nature is pure. Our inner compass mirrors the intention of our true self. However, we tend to increasingly discount our intuition and sense of knowing during our childhood, adolescence and adulthood in order to fit in or conform. We create an unauthentic mask. Don't berate yourself over this; it happens to the best of us. Therefore, within us, rises the lifelong mind chatter of "I'm not good enough," which leads us to repeatedly undermine ourselves as adults. Wearing an artificial mask while denying our true selves has its roots mostly in our upbringing and our acceptance of other people's perception of us.

We also notice that young children naturally have a strong desire to contribute, to be challenged by worthy goals, and to be productive. Initially, they see the connectivity and unity of everything, and the literal impact of communications and situations, but then we program them to ignore these innate abilities. Let us for a moment, think about what would happen if we refused to give in to the desire to program young people so much? How can we maintain their natural curiosity and restore our own?

*The heart is naturally radiant;
defilements are only visitors. – Buddha*

Fundamentally our essence is noble and pure. However, society and parental pressures, worldly desires, inclinations, the shadow side of our ego and ignorance (lack of knowledge) create veils between our true essence and its expression in the physical world. As we grow in enlightenment and awareness, our mission in life should be to remove the veils that we have acquired over the years.

To open our heart and eliminate the mind chatter and the "visitors" that the Buddha referred to, we need to be vigilant in our quest to understand our programming so we can regain our natural curiosity and insight.

Meaning of Wisdom

*The only true wisdom is
in knowing you know nothing.* — Socrates

FELORA ZIARI

A wise person knows not many things, just fewer things that aren't true. — Anonymous

What is wisdom? Why do we need it? How does it impact our life?

Wisdom is not just good information or sage advice we receive or give, nor is it limited to personal experience and observation. Neither is it common sense. Common sense does not really exist because what is common or normal to one person may be completely different to another. *Common sense is an overused and misused term that comes from filtering the prejudices of others through our own opinion and understanding.*

> *As millions of us discover our special genius and learn to leverage the genius of others, we will learn to celebrate the diversity of ideas rather than argue about who is right.*

Wisdom is the combination of the innate knowledge that was infused into us by the divine blueprint of creation, and the teachings from our life experiences. The alchemy of this process might be referred to as "our unique path." Combine our one-of-a-kind wisdom with free will and we have a special blend of genius.

As millions of us discover our special genius and learn to leverage the genius of others, we will learn to celebrate the diversity of ideas rather than argue about who is right. Really listening with the intention of learning puts us on a trajectory to live our lives with our true self aligned with inner wisdom.

It is not the breadth of our knowledge that makes us wise, rather it is how we use that knowledge in discerning the truth. Wisdom endows us with the ability to discern the truth in order for us to choose the right path for the right reason. When we apply wisdom to our decisions, we are guided by the lamp of divine guidance that lights up our path.

Humility

Humility is very misunderstood. Our shadow self limits our understanding of humility. Humility is not the opposite of vanity, pride or egotism. Instead, it is about letting go of pride and allowing our higher nature to guide us. Leaders are considered most successful when they are authentically humble, and not attached to power and ego; their actions are based on serving the greater good. Hence they are not afraid of letting go of their power or influence. They lead by doing the right thing for the right reason instead of what others expect from them or what gets them ahead.

> *Really listening with the intention of learning puts us on a trajectory to live our lives with our true self aligned with our inner wisdom.*

A young man heard about Jalál ad-Dín Rúmí, a Sufi poet and scholar of the thirteenth century whose wisdom and spiritual insight was sought by many. This young man set out to find Rúmí so he could understand the mystery of life better. He walked for days and finally arrived at his destination where he saw an old man approaching. He recognized this old man to be Rúmí himself. He prostrated himself, putting his head on the ground in front of this revered philosopher. When he looked up, he saw that Rúmí had also prostrated himself before him. After few rounds of prostration from both sides, the young man asked Rumi, *Why would such a scholar of religion and spirituality bend down and prostrate himself before an ordinary man?* Rúmí answered, *Why shouldn't I prostrate myself before a servant of my Beloved?*

The lesson being pointed out here is that humility is not about thinking of ourselves as being less than others; it is seeing the greatness inherent in others, and recognizing the potential for greatness in others. Humility is to be a witness to the innate nobility of every person who crosses our path.

How do we increase our level of humility? First, we need to communicate with others with the intent of learning from them, and not with the aim of producing a better argument or attain the upper hand in a conversation. To truly practice this virtue, we need to have a strong sense of our values and have a firm grasp of who we are. While silently celebrating our own gifts, qualities, and achievements, we admire other people's gifts and greatness without considering ourselves as superior. When we approach this state, we have begun to practice humility.

The Code

CHAPTER 5
EXTRINSIC ASPECTS OF SELF

Shadow Ego

Ego is very much misunderstood. Ego can be defined as your awareness of your own self or your own identity. The Concise Oxford Dictionary defines 'ego' as 'the conscious thinking self'. The Cambridge dictionary defines it as "The idea or opinion that you have of yourself. The level of your ability and intelligence and your importance as a person." The origin of the word *ego* is from the Latin word for "I." Having an ego is the only way to know that each one of us "exists" on earth as an individual. Ego allows us to interact in relation to others.

When the ego is expressed from a place of negative emotions and impulses like; arrogance, greed, jealousy, and suppressed desires, it is called the *shadow ego*. Carl Jung defines the shadow ego as all the aspects of your personality that have been rejected by the ego.

Carl Jung stated the shadow to be "the unknown dark side of the personality." According to Jung, the shadow is susceptible to psychological projection in which we defend ourselves against our own unconscious impulses or qualities (both positive and negative) by denying their existence in ourselves while attributing them to others.[1]

As mentioned before, while growing up, we were either rewarded or punished for our behavior. In order to survive, to please others or be loved, we suppressed certain aspects of ourselves. As adults, these suppressed aspects show up as negative emotions or reactions. When we are triggered, our shadow ego shows up and projects our suppressed aspects unto others. For example, if we have suppressed our natural assertiveness, we may become judgmental or angry when someone else is assertive.

Understanding such emotional triggers can help us understand our shadow ego and manage the triggers more effectively.

Self-sabotage

Self-sabotage results from an internal emotional struggle between who we really are and the false persona that we have adopted to survive. Although the struggle can take many different forms, it retards or prevents the achievement of our goals and desires. Without a clear roadmap to our personal, unique requirements for fulfillment, the probability of self-sabotage is high. To a person without self-mastery, the

---

[1] See https://en.wikipedia.org/wiki/Psychological_projection

failure to meet their goals usually involves circumstances that seem out of their control. We can recall so many familiar names of people who gained huge success in one area yet had to deal with severe problems in another. How many wealthy movie stars or business people have had disastrous marriages or problems with alcohol or drugs? What causes this? Of what use is personal power if we are building a life around someone else's agenda? Why accomplish someone else's goals instead of our own?

Women generally sabotage themselves by wanting to be 100% accurate and perfectionist before they execute an idea. One of the reasons is that women are less likely to take risks when compared to men. An analysis[2] performed by Byrnes, Miller, and Schafer (1999) reviewed over 150 papers on gender differences in risk perception and concluded that the literature "clearly" indicated, "male participants are more likely to take risks than female participants."

We learn to self-sabotage at an early age. Dr. Heidi Grant Halvorson, author of *Succeed: How We Can Reach Our Goals*[3], compared the way bright girls and boys responded when given something complex and challenging.

She found that smart girls were quick to surrender and give up when they were asked to solve a complex problem with which they were unfamiliar.

---

2 Byrnes, James P.; Miller, David C.; Schafer, William D., Gender *Differences in Risk Taking: a meta analysis*, Psychological Bulletin 125(3):367-383, May 1999

3 Halverson, Heidi G., *Succeed: How We Can Reach Our Goals*, Hudson Street Press, 2010.

Surprisingly, the higher the girl's IQ, the more likely she was to give up. Smart boys, on the other hand, looked at the complexity of the problem as a challenge, and found it invigorating. They were more apt to increase their focus to solve the problem.[4]

At the 5th grade level, girls performed much better than boys in almost every subject. However when girls were given difficult material, they handled it differently than boys. *Bright girls were much quicker to doubt their ability, to lose confidence, and to become less effective learners as a result.*

Researchers believe that *bright girls believe that their abilities are innate and unchangeable, while bright boys believe that they can develop ability through effort and practice.*

So why is that? Our belief systems develop throughout childhood. We are taught to think and behave in a certain way depending on our gender, our culture and the community where we grew up. The gender difference is surely because girls are often taught to be more cautious than boys. They are discouraged from taking risks.

In reality, self-sabotage is a battle between our lower nature and our higher nature. Because our lower nature is based on our shadow ego, fears and mortality, it needs to be transformed in order for us to develop awareness and be able to access our higher nature. When we avoid listening to our desires, we

---

4 From: http://www.psychologytoday.com/blog/the-science-success/201101/the-trouble-bright-girls

create uncertainty in our lives. The byproduct of uncertainty is fear, pain, grief and sadness. We become a divided self.

What Do I Need?

Beyond the question of "what do I want?" is another, perhaps more important question, "what do I need?" There is much confusion between what we want and what we need. A need is something required for survival, such as food, air, and shelter. A want, on the other hand, is not what we need to survive; rather it's what we feel would make our lives better.

When we convince ourselves that our "wants" are our "needs," we create disparity in our life. The biggest problem is when we define an emotional connection as a need to survive or be happy. For example, I may believe that, in order to be happy, I require a loving partner who is a better communicator. This "want" repackaged as a "need" creates a sense of entitlement. We then feel entitled to demand it because we believe that's what we need to survive.

Most of our wants are not needs. Distinguishing between *needs* and *wants* can help us manage our expectations and put things in perspective. We will be less frustrated if we accept that many of our "wants" are not necessary for our survival. Life becomes less stressful.

The Code

CHAPTER 6
PREREQUISITES FOR SELF-MASTERY

Energy Integration vs. Energy Drains

The art of manifesting what we desire requires that our thoughts and actions be aligned with our vision. With such an alignment, less energy is required to manifest our goals and less energy is wasted on counterproductive activities.

Manifestation requires energy. To be successful in our personal or professional lives, we need to increase the energy of integration and lower the energy drains. In other words, to manifest what we want, we need to make sure that the integration

> *... to manifest what we want, we need to make sure that the integration energy, the energy we are putting into the system — into our goals and vision — is greater than the energy leaving the system.*

energy, the energy we are putting into the system—into our goals and vision—is greater than the energy leaving the system.

Without a doubt, energy is the foundation of personal interaction. According to physics, everything we encounter is a system. Human beings as well as organizations and businesses are systems; and every system requires energy to function. In physics, the first and second laws of thermodynamics describe how energy is used in a system. Energy is the amount of work or the amount of the forces that push or pull on an object.

The first law of thermodynamics is called conservation, which means that the amount of potential energy or energy integration to a system is finite and fixed. Energy integration, commonly referred to as high energy, comes from things that are fun, positive, and have a high vibration. We know many people that have high energy personalities—so much energy that they are able to boost other people's energy levels.

The second law of thermodynamics is called entropy, which states that everything will eventually disintegrate. Entropy is like energy drains. There are people that have low energy personalities. When we are around them, we feel drained, exhausted or sad. Low energy feels negative, frantic and chaotic.

It is not just negative or mean people that are energy drains. Situations and emotions can sap our energy. We can feel drained when we watch a negatively charged movie. A weak mental or emotional state is an energy drain or entropy. When people go through difficult situations, or are angry and bitter, they have less energy to be effective. When we are sick, we need more energy to maintain the body and that is why we are told to rest, to conserve our energy so we can heal. The quantity and quality of food we consume can contribute to or diminish our available energy.

Awareness of energy integration and energy drains can help us be more intentional in the way we engage with others so that we avoid losing energy. A good way of doing this would be through the creation of situations or dialogues that are high in integration and low in entropy. Some of the biggest energy drains are our thoughts and negative self-talk. We all hear people say, "I am tired of thinking." The thinking process is very complex and requires energy. Negative thoughts require even more energy and can deplete vitality, making us tired.

We can be intentional about our energy level and increase the integration by tapping into something that makes us happy. Psychologists believe that even a pretend smile can boost our energy and change our moods. Other great sources of energy are sleep, meditation, creative or inspirational activities, and positive conversations. In Taoism, there are a series of practices such as meditation and Qigong (Internal Energy Cultivation) that help individuals learn to increase their internal energy by releasing the tensions, reducing the stress and being at peace with themselves. These practices help the individual to seek the truth and free themselves from emotions that drain their energy.

We each have the capacity to open the gateway of our heart and be full of energy when we need a boost. We may see a movie that inspires positive thoughts, causing an idea to come to our mind that keeps us awake all night working on the idea. Below are some activities that will help you maintain a higher level of energy.

- Pay attention to your mind-chatter and stop yourself from going on the downward spiral with negative self-talk. Listen to what your mind tells you and take two actions that can either calm your mind or help you solve the anxiety created by the negative self-talk.
- Check in with yourself regularly to identify your current energy level and the source of energy drains. Create a plan to consciously change your energy level, even if you can only fake a smile.
- Increase energy integration by breathing deeply and exercising.
- When you feel low in energy, close your eyes and meditate for a few minutes.
- Practice 20-30 minutes of daily meditation.
- Get enough sleep.
- Stop thinking about past experiences or mistakes and forgive yourself using positive affirmations.

- Each day, look for inspirational activities or quotes that can enhance your mood
- More importantly, do things that makes you happy and stop doing things that makes you unhappy by asking yourself, Is this bringing me joy?

Our Programming & Our Choices

Imagine if Picasso had been able to show his famous paintings to his art teacher when he was six years old. His teacher would surely have said, "Those are terrible. You have no future in art!" The standards accept as a child are determined by the limitations of the authority figures we respect, forcing us to squash our unique desires that emerge during those years of childhood and young adulthood. We are told to be reasonable, be practical, and most importantly, do not disappoint.

We are fortunate that in this day and age, we have the technology to access unlimited information about any topic without relying on a single source such as a school, parent, or politician. This independence lowers the control of those who influenced society in the past. Form follows function, and information is now beginning to follow people's curiosity instead of being limited by the programming.

Prior to the internet, powerful people decided what books would be printed, what would be taught in schools or preached in churches. Today, anyone can find many answers to any of life's great questions. Information is no longer in small streams flowing down from ideological mountains; it is an ocean of information where anyone can go for a broad selection of answers at any time.

Even though we now have an ocean of information, most schools are still teaching according to the old model that many of us experienced as children. Most of us remember sitting in rows of desks at school and being told when we can go to the bathroom, what to think, and how to think. Over time, our wishes and creativity were hidden away in a box. As students, our role models were adults and when they said, "It is," we accepted it. We were then constrained by a smaller domain of what was possible according to the realm of the teacher.

Another influence on our beliefs is the media. Instead of presenting a holistic, pragmatic approach, the ever-present media persistently presents a black-white, right-wrong view that firmly plants a sense of duality and separation (us vs. them) in our consciousness.

In today's politics, many people do not know what to believe. They are brainwashed by politicians and political commentators on both the right and the left. People who have not experienced a broad range of views tend to accept everything they hear as facts and do not read between the lines. They become followers because it is easier than researching the facts and then thinking for themselves. They spend their energy attacking the other side rather than finding common ground or solutions to the problems.

There is a real danger when we follow others without

thinking for ourselves. In the Bahá'í Faith, people are encouraged to practice "independent investigation of the truth" where, instead of blindly following others, they acquire knowledge "with their own eyes and not through the eyes of others." Indeed, engaging in a personal search for truth is the only way for us to understand the "why" behind our actions and to make an effective effort to put our desires into practice.

If we are going to pursue our goals effectively, our actions must be based on facts, not on what we wish were true. Brainwashed people live in a black and white world of us vs. them. In their mind, "those other people" are the cause of all our problems. This is not reality; this is fear and ego projected onto a world that is much more nuanced, where everyone is doing the best they can to care for their families. If we want to make the best choices—choices that will enable us to achieve our goals—we must strip away any distorting ideas that may have crept into us from media, culture or authority figures. We must see reality—as it is with no distortion—"through our own eyes and not the eyes of others."

> *We must see reality as it is with no distortion – "through our own eyes and not the eyes of others."*

Would you rather be right, or have results?

Healthy Boundaries

Boundaries provide us with the ability to function as independent people. Within those healthy boundaries, our relationships will have a chance to grow and flourish. Most of us were raised in families of origin with at least some level of dysfunction and with a poor set of boundaries. In many families, conflict is habitually avoided even though unresolved anxiety and conflict are present, leading to ongoing sadness, anger, and other challenges.

Many of us were unknowingly desensitized to our family drama through continual exposure to the drama in TV and movies. We listened to decades of songs that follow one of several predictable themes of self-pity. Cultural factors, combined with a person's upbringing, are an extremely powerful blend that results in weakened boundaries and a distorted self-image.

The act of fulfilling our desires requires that we consciously examine and create healthy boundaries. We start the examination by having a clear understanding of ourselves and of what makes us unique. Taking this step allows us to remain who we truly are inside long-term relationships in which each party empowers the other. These co-empowered relationships support our process of upgrading our self-mastery and moving along our spiritual path. Having a sense of our new Self allows us to clearly communicate our needs and desires without making any other person responsible for our progress along the path. We want to respect the boundaries of our partner and other people, as they respect ours.

Learning what this process requires is worth the conscious effort, but it can be tricky. Consider Carla, who said, "I tell my husband all the time what I want, with great specificity, but he seems to forget my needs or he puts them at the bottom of his priority list." Carla considered her husband responsible for her happiness. She will learn to take responsibility and share her plans with her husband. Everyone has free will, including Carla's husband.

The only way to get a conscious relationship off the ground is to be responsible and co-empowered, not blaming and co-dependent. As Carla grew up, she may have lacked the support she needed to form a healthy sense of her own identity. She may have learned that to get her way with others, she had to intrude on their boundaries and force an outcome.

Having a strong but fluid relationship with our identity enables us to welcome the expanding knowledge of our higher self and of our shadow ego. As we expand our ability to love all the aspects of ourselves, we find that we have an increasing appreciation for the unique qualities of others, leading to more satisfying intimacy. While similarities between two people might bring them together initially, it is their differences that contribute to their mutual self-actualization and long-term friendship.

> *Celebrating the contrasts within healthy boundaries provides balance in a world that rewards diversity.*

In healthy relationships, there can be unity in diversity. Finding out who we are and what makes us unique, and then doing the same with others, allows us to rejoice in a process of discovery that is never-ending. Self-mastery enables us to realize that our values are not dependent on anyone else. We understand that no one—not our family, friends, not even our significant other—is required to replicate our values exactly. They need to respect our values as we respect theirs. Celebrating the contrasts within healthy boundaries provides balance in a world that rewards diversity. When people come to their values by choice instead of cultural programming, everyone becomes more powerful.

How Does Transformation Happen?

We are products of many influences. We awaken our true nature when we objectively evaluate the influences that informed our beliefs and actions. We need to separate the influences that hold us back from those that keep us motivated. Our growing self-awareness will transform us, propelling us forward as we use each new experience to reinforce our new vision while discarding the beliefs that no longer serve us.

Over the years, many books have been written on personal transformation. Most of them use the words *change* and *transformation* interchangeably. In my opinion change means that the original version of us was not good enough, so we have to become someone else. However, *transformation* does not deny our past. It is about *reform*, like making a beautiful ceramic bowl from a lump of clay. It is still clay, yet we are shaping it into a new and improved form of itself.

One of the most powerful explanations I have heard was that of Lynne Twist, an award-winning author who wrote *The Soul of Money*[5]. This is an extract from the graduation speech she gave at Bainbridge Graduate Institute in June 2012.

> *Change is volatile. Transformation is completely different – though sometimes it is called change. Transformation never makes the past wrong. It transforms it. It does not deny it. It honors it in a way that you can move forward without making anything wrong, and having the past somehow now become complete, rather than wrong. Transformation has a permanence to it – where once you transform, once you awaken, once you see the stations you did not see before, you cannot go back. Transformation has the ultimate power of time, and what the world is crying for now is transformation, not necessarily more change, though some change may be a part of it, the route to transformation. Transformation suddenly makes the past make sense, and new futures open up.* — Lynne Twist

Transformation is similar to eating habits. If we know a certain food is good for us, how do we keep the love of this healthy food alive? When

> *Transformation has to become a habit, a way of being that does not happen to us; rather it is created by us.*

---

5 Twist, Lynne, *The Soul of Money: reclaiming the wealth of our inner resources*, W. W. Norton & Company; 2006.

we know the food is making a difference in how our body functions, even if we do not see an immediate result, we continue eating healthier. Transformation has to become a habit, a way of being that does not happen to us; rather it is created by us. Effective transformation is about progress and expansion. We need to shift the present state to a new expanded state by developing a new mindset and new habits.

Gandhi talks about our belief as the starting point in our journey of personal transformation. He said that our belief creates our thoughts and our thoughts drive our actions, which ultimately decides our destiny.

> *Your beliefs become your thoughts, Your thoughts become your words, Your words become your actions, Your actions become your habits, Your habits become your values, Your values become your destiny.* — Mahatma Gandhi

Even when the desire for self-mastery is strong and we are able to visualize the life we desire, we can only achieve great outcomes if we create a passion for transformation—a passion powerful enough to guide and drive all our actions. When we are passionate about our transformation, we are able to endure any challenges. We do not give up easily. In order to create sufficient passion for transformation, we need to first establish a state of emotional balance. We achieve that balance by simultaneously letting go of our self-limitations, keeping our ego in check, and creating new values and new habits that support the desired outcome.

FELORA ZIARI

UNIT 3
CULTIVATE

The Code

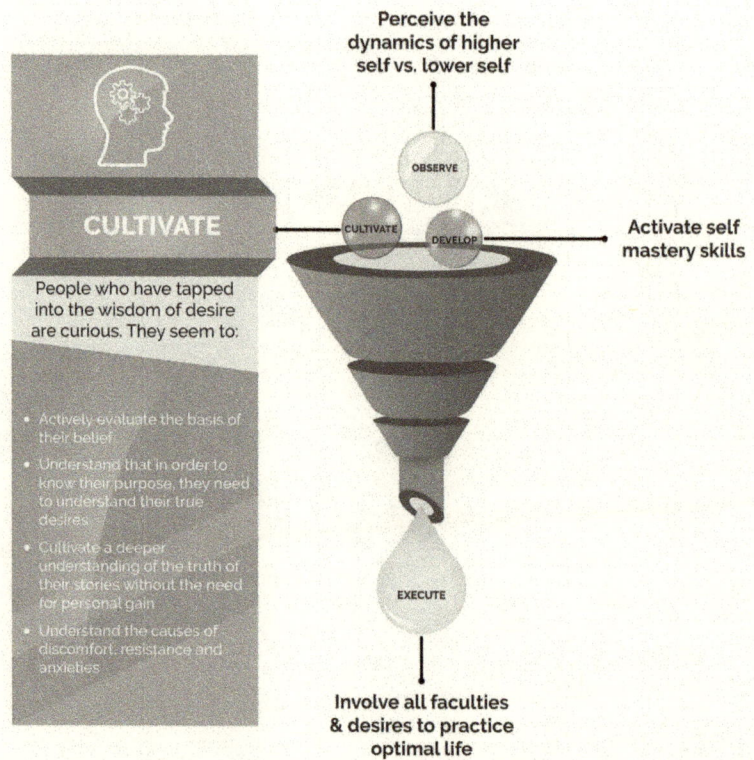

CHAPTER 7
SELF-MASTERY

What are the attributes of Self-Mastery?

What are the attributes of a person who has understood and practices "self-mastery"? When you meet someone who has mastered their Self, what strikes you? In what ways do they behave differently than the rest of us?

Self-mastery is a process that is not complete when we understand what it means. People that have learned the practice of self-mastery see the results of their actions, good or not-so-good, as feedback.

> *People who have learned the practice of self-mastery see the results of their actions, good or not-so-good, as feedback.*

Success starts with knowing ourselves. Self-Mastery is possibly the greatest achievement of our life.

The Code

*If you do not conquer self,
you will be conquered by self. – Napoleon Hill.*

The first step, and one of the most important steps in this journey, is awareness. Awareness involves having an understanding of our strengths, weaknesses, fears, values, and our core belief system. *When we master self-awareness, we do not allow the outside world to influence our emotional response or our choices; rather, we rely on our inner wisdom and knowing to create balance and harmony between our inner state and our environment.* When we add the ingredient of self-love to self-awareness, we are at peace with ourselves; we accept ourselves as we are without any form of self-judgment or self-criticism.

Here are some attributes of people who practice self-mastery:

- They have awareness and understanding of their desires.
- They know the shadow side of their ego and know how it can get triggered.
- They have great empathy and compassion for other people.
- They are able to feel their emotions, reflect on the cause of negative emotions and then release them.
- They are grateful for who they are, what they have, and what they have accomplished.
- They are unassuming and humble.

- They are aware of their shortcomings.
- They determine the truth for themselves.
- They don't make assumptions.
- They have unwavering integrity and high moral values.

With self-mastery, we know exactly who we are; we know our moral values, principles and our beliefs. One of my mantras that has always helped me remain grounded regardless of life's circumstances is this: *I am who I am regardless of who you are or what life presents.*

> *I am who I am regardless of who you are or what life presents.*

A path in the woods

In *The Book of Awakening*[6], Mark Nepo writes a beautiful account where, through a dream, Carl Jung describes self-discovery and our relationship to our soul:

> *Carl Jung had a dream that he was cutting a path in the woods, unsure where it was leading, but working hard at it nonetheless. Tired and sweating, he came upon a cabin in a clearing. He dropped his tools and approached the cabin. Through the window he saw a being in prayer at a simple altar. The door was open and Jung went in. As he drew closer, he realized that the being in*

---
6 Nepo, Mark, *The Book of Awakening: Having the Life You Want by Being Present to the Life You Have*, Conari Press, 2000.

prayer was himself and that his life of cutting a path was this being's dream. ...

Without knowing it, we, like Jung, work hard at cutting a path to our deeper self that waits patiently for us to arrive, all tired, aching, and out of breath. Once that path is cleared and once the being at our center is discovered, we can return to the world in relationship with our soul. We can discover a deeper, more peaceful sense of home.

The path to self-mastery and self-discovery is a lifelong journey. The path is never straight; there are milestones and turns waiting for us. At each juncture, we learn something new about ourselves. We move from one chapter of our life's book to a new chapter. Along the way, we make life choices that will lead us to discover a greater and more meaningful aspect of our core.

Who Owns Our Life?

Our choices have the power to build, but they can also destroy. Conscious choices can influence our lives so that we are awakened to a new level of existence. There is a fascinating story of Buckminster Fuller that shows us how the power of choice can influence our lives. When Buckminster Fuller was in his early thirties, he had several unfortunate incidents that drove him to the verge of suicide. He was jobless and had just lost his son. In desperation, he decided that life was meaningless and he did not wish to live anymore.

As he stood on the shore of Lake Michigan deciding whether to end his life, he had an awakening, a vision. He realized at that moment, as he considered drowning himself in the lake, that in reality his life did not belong to him but to the universe. Buckminster Fuller decided to choose life. Buckminster Fuller embarked on what he called "an experiment to discover what the little, penniless, unknown individual might be able to do effectively on behalf of all humanity." The rest of his life was dedicated to answering the question, "Does humanity have a chance to survive lastingly and successfully on planet Earth, and if so, how?" Throughout the course of his remaining life, Fuller was awarded twenty-eight patents, authored twenty-eight books, and received forty-seven honorary degrees. For an individual who almost committed suicide, that is outstanding.

To discern what choices you are making, answer the following powerful questions:

- Who owns my life?
- Who can I become so I can have a greater, more positive impact?

When I almost drowned in the well, I perceived a different experience of my existence that was not based on what I could see, rather what I felt and what I chose to do after my experience.

> *Life is easy; it's how we manage our experiences that makes our lives difficult.*

The Code

You see, life is easy; it's how we manage our experiences that makes our lives difficult. The choice to make our lives easy or hard is ultimately ours and ours alone!

CHAPTER 8
LOOKING BEYOND THE ILLUSION

Living at the Resonant Frequency

Einstein says it best:

> *Match the frequency of the reality you want and you cannot help but get that reality. It can be no other way. This is not philosophy. This is physics.*
> — *Albert Einstein*

In Martial Arts, there is a practice called *Wei Wu Wei*, which means "action without action" or, in other words, non-doing. An important concept in Taoism, Wei Wu Wei suggests effortless action, a state in which you consciously release control so that you are aligned with the flow of life. For example, happiness is not something you find or you seek; rather, it is the byproduct of doing the things that make you happy.

The concept of "living at the resonant frequency" is similar to the practice of Wei Wu Wei. The challenge is to know our personal truth—to look beyond the illusion. This challenge varies among the different generations alive today. Many people have observed that the newer generations have a different awareness of struggling and striving. Younger people are embracing thriving as their natural state. They "just don't get it" when it comes to the paradigm of previous generations who were programmed to conform by a culture, an education system, or perhaps a religion. As we live our lives based on the concept of thriving as a natural state of being, we create emotional stability, balance and harmony. Living at the resonant frequency is the cultivation of a state of being that enables us to effortlessly respond to the challenges, circumstances and situations that arise in our life.

We have to remember that *thriving does not mean being busy.* The following quote is attributed to Ernest Hemingway, "Never mistake motion for action." Many people fall short of achieving their desired results because they are frenetic, constantly busy, while filling their lives with many actions that do not lead to their optimal goals. Such *too-busy* people are often responding to external demands that keep them away from their primary desires and objectives. That is the challenge of the generations that confuse busy-ness with results. The practice of Wei Wu Wei is an effortless movement and pursuit that results in life unfolding in accordance with its divine purpose because our actions are based on our desires and passion.

How Do We Interpret Our Reality?

Desire is an innate aspect of every human being, and is the fuel that ignites the passion for creating magical outcomes in our lives. Desire can be viewed as a sense of longing, yearning, craving, or need. Some scholars view it as a chemical or hormonal phenomenon, while others attach a stigma to desire as something destructive—perhaps due to the prevalence of addiction and the "more is better" attitude in our culture. Jung explained that an addiction is "the spiritual thirst of our being for wholeness," and "Addiction is related to a normal human drive toward wholeness which has gone awry." Besides addiction, another result of a normal desire gone awry is the systematic obstruction of the desires of others. We will get to that later.

What do we believe about who we are and about our place in the world? Where do these beliefs come from? What do we believe about others? And why do we believe that? In order to really understand ourselves, we need to understand how we look at the reality of the world around us and how we interpret what we see. Our beliefs about our identity, about the world, about relationships, and about others are rooted in many different factors. Our society, culture, family, and childhood experiences have influenced our outlook. Any of these distorted beliefs or perspectives can hinder our understanding of the truth.

Reality—what is real and true—exists completely independent of us. Our perception of that reality depends on how objectively we are able to look at it.

For each individual, the subjective interpretation of the various elements of our experience influences our perception of the overall reality. The accuracy of that perception will vary greatly from person to person. As we understand our values and ourselves better, our knowledge broadens and we gain a keener understanding of our perceptions and their limitations. For instance, if I know I have a prejudice toward a group of people because of my upbringing, when I meet one of those people, I can make the mental adjustment to discredit the prejudice and treat the person with respect.

Besides religious beliefs, most of our beliefs about our identity are formed when we have experiences that cause a strong emotional reaction. These emotional experiences create beliefs that become deeply ingrained in us. Most of my coaching clients find that much of what they believe about themselves is rooted in childhood and early adolescence.

One of my clients told me that whenever she did not finish a business project on time, or was late to a meeting, she felt shame which created anxiety in her and caused further problems in her interactions with others and even caused her to become ill. When we looked for a possible root cause of the problem, she remembered that when she was in elementary school, a teacher embarrassed her in front of the class for not completing a task. As she vividly remembered the embarrassment and shame, she realized that her sense of shame had stayed with her throughout her life. Later as an adult, she had a belief system that she was not good enough and so could not do a good job. As a result, when she failed to finish her work assignments on time, she felt the same emotional sensations as she did in her elementary class.

When you have clarity and awareness of the sources of your personal beliefs, you do not give these beliefs any more power. Furthermore, you need to look at the habits that have been formed on the basis of those beliefs. Otherwise you will respond to the situation the same way as before.

Jean Houston, in her book, *A Mythic Life: Learning to Live our Greater Story*[7], refers to four principles that most people have used to create their reality:

- The first principle is the *Physical Reality*: the facts around the incident, the who, what, where and when without engaging our belief system, emotions or interpretations.

- The second principle is the *Psychological Reality*: the facts based on our skills of discernment (the ability to Judge well), which includes our knowledge and wisdom to understand the meaning of the physical experience.

- The third one is the *Mythic Reality*: how the incident relates to the rest of our life and our past experiences. As a result, we may generalize when the same thing is repeated; we might say it "always" happens. If an expected,

---
7 Houston, Jean, *A Mythic Life: Learning to Live our Greater Story*, Harper, San Francisco, 1996.

positive event fails to occur, we read into this that it "never" happens.

- The fourth principle is the *Essential Reality*: where the concepts of cultural values, expectations and personal values define the experiences of the situation.

Is perception a reality? Does the way we interpret things change if we change our perception of it? Culture, media, relationships, mindset and internal conversations—moment to moment—influence the context of perception.

In India there is an ancient story in which six blind men were asked to determine what an elephant looked like by feeling different parts of the elephant's body. The blind man who felt a leg said the elephant is like a pillar; the one who felt the tail said the elephant is like a rope; the one who felt the trunk said the elephant is like a tree branch; the one who felt the ear said the elephant is like a hand fan; the one who felt the belly said the elephant is like a wall; and the one who felt the tusk said the elephant is like a solid pipe.

Often, like the blind men touching the elephant, we are blinded by our limited perception of the situation because we have failed to grasp the context in its entirety. What we believe and perceive about our world and our role in it, impacts how we live our life and it influences the outcome of our vision.

The following questions can help us get more clarity about our perception of the reality:

- What beliefs do I hold about myself?
- Why do I believe that?
- What are the impact of these beliefs?
- What habits did I form in order to compensate for those beliefs?
- How can I change these habits?
- What would be my mantra that could counteract the false beliefs I have about myself?

To create clarity, we need to let our thoughts and emotions pass through us without judgment. We do not want them to linger, nor do we want to attach any story to them. Attachment to these less-than-true stories distorts our perception of reality. Studies have shown that our minds can be selective in interpreting the information. While failing to see facts that conflict with our limited understanding, we absorb other information that supports what we believe or what we know based on our personal biases, judgments, experiences, etc. In other words, our focus, understanding and perceptions are limited; and therefore, at times, we filter out valid information based on our prejudices. While filtering out positive details, we may be magnifying the negative aspects of

> *To create clarity, we need to give permission to our thoughts and emotions, allowing them to pass through us without judgment.*

a situation. At other times, we do the opposite and focus our attention on the positive while filtering out the negative aspects of the situation.

We see what we want to see.

To be realistic, we need to consider that there are always two sides to any story, situation or information. As we learn to be more accepting of situations, we will learn to let go of resistance and reactive patterns. We will become neutral and see the truth for what it is without our distorted perception of it.

Our Masks as Programmed Conformity

Look for invitations, not validations. Invitations are a cause for growth. Validations, enhance our delusional masks!

We live in a world that calls for programmed conformity. Society sometimes resents uniqueness and, at other times, rewards it. Society claims to value overachievement, but we teach school according to standardized testing, teaching kids what to think instead of how to think. We dull their curiosity, teaching them that the dates and outcomes of battles are more important milestones in history than understanding human nature. How sad is that?

Expressing our uniqueness while simultaneously obeying the demand for conformity creates what is known as a double bind, or paradox. Sometimes, this paradox creates dichotomy, conflict and imbalance—at both an individual and societal level. Hence, it is imperative that we are aware of our heart's desire and listen to our inner knowing at all times; they provide a roadmap that allows our extraordinary gifts to be expressed as well as our lives to be lived with much more ease and grace. The alternative to pursuing our desires is to succumb to the negative energy caused by self-denial, leaving our voices unexpressed, and our gifts withheld from the world.

Let us look at some of the façades or masks we may have been wearing in order to conform to our environment, make us feel more important or simply be able to fit in:

- Even though we are innately introverted, we pretend to be funny and outgoing. We work very hard to remember jokes. We do this in spite of our natural inclination to solitude.
- We pretend to be overly enthusiastic about certain issues (like politics), because we believe being passionate will get us noticed, or people will perceive us as smart.
- We try to be very caring because we want to be seen as compassionate people, even though in our private lives we show our kindness and caring through other means.
- We show off our knowledge in order to come across as intellectual.

When we are portraying a false self, we are disconnected from our higher self. On a deeper level, we are trying too hard to prove that we are worth knowing instead of *believing* that we are worth knowing. We self-sabotage ourselves and our growth when we pretend to be different than who we truly are. We are swimming upstream and against the current. When we are being true to ourselves, we accept and celebrate ourselves.

When we are aligned with our true calling and purpose, our work inspires others. When we are in our power, we create an opening for other people's light to shine through as well.

> *Are we trying too hard to prove that we are worth knowing instead of believing that we are worth knowing?*

How great the joy that is experienced when we share our gifts with others! *Light attracts, inspires and motivates light.* When we abandon our desire, we close down the channel of inspiration; the fire of our passion dims and our heart's song does not create the vibrational joy. If we fail to follow our desires, we do not accomplish what has been destined for us. We betray our commitment to our higher self. To excel at anything, we must tap into our deep-rooted inspiration and passion.

Removing Our Masks

In most of our human relationships, we spend much of our time reassuring one another that our costumes of identity are on straight.
— Ram Dass

One way of looking at the corruption of our childhood innocence or building false belief systems is the analogy of masks. We learn early in life to hide our real selves. This is especially true of women. Rather than be our true self, our parents and society ask us to blend in and accept their standards and values. They may be trying to protect us so we do not get hurt, or maybe because that was the only way they knew to raise children. In order to avoid pain or conflict, we put on a virtual mask so we could fit in, be accepted and acknowledged.

However after some time, we lose ourselves in the fiction that we created. The mask becomes our delusion. We convince ourselves that we are the mask. As part of our delusion, the masks define our preferences and our goals, which may have little to do with what we truly want. Our distorted preferences are not aligned with our divine purpose and therefore our actions contradict our innate knowing, producing stress.

> *The greatest battle we face as human beings is the battle to protect our true selves from the self the world wants us to become.*
> *— E. E. Cummings*

Our transformation cannot happen until we understand what masks we are wearing. Awareness alone is not enough, we need to remove these masks, or at least understand why we are wearing them. Once we have clarity about our true identity, and understand who we truly are, then our lives will improve exponentially. We will begin to make better choices that are aligned with our higher purpose. One of the most important aspects of transformation is gaining an understanding of how to make choices in order to implement the goals that unfold from our new self-awareness. Decision theorists tell us that we are always making choices between different options. These choices flow from our preferences, which, at the moment, may be defined by our mask rather than our reality. When our choices are based on our perception of ourselves, they might be reactive instead of being proactive based on integrity, values and our higher purpose.

I realized that one of the masks I was wearing was the need to please people. I would say yes when I meant no, I would agree when in reality I disagreed. It then dawned on me that this was a cultural behavior that I learned growing up in Middle East. We were taught to be courteous to others. However, as a child I didn't learn that being courteous and considerate didn't mean denying my own belief. I didn't know that I was forgoing some aspect of my well-being; rather, I thought I was being humble and polite. This people-pleasing behavior also created other habits such as the avoidance of conflicts. I realized that I was sacrificing my ideologies and happiness in order to come across as courteous and a humble individual. In time, I have been able to realize that authenticity is the same as truthfulness. When we are truthful to ourselves we practice the highest form of self-love and self-respect. I was able to break this habit by simply asking myself, "What is the truth?"

When we make decisions, our higher nature or our noble self reflects on truth while our lower nature reflects on the shadow side of ego and self-gratification. We all have access to the noble self when we make decisions. In order to make the right choice between different options, we need to tap into our higher nature and our inner knowing for guidance while asking the right questions, such as: Is this option for my highest good?

My own life experiences led me to believe that there are two powerful tools that are essential for true awareness: love and detachment. Love is the magnet that holds every aspect of life together. Here, I am not referring to romantic love. This is a Divine Love instilled in every human being that can flow through us to everything and everyone around us. It creates unity of purpose and guides us to make meaningful choices. Detachment, on the other hand, is putting the Divine Will above our Will. It enables us to let go of worldly desires that hold us back so that we are able to let the Divine into our lives where our choices will be based on integrity, leading to the highest good for us and for everyone else involved.

> *Love is the water of life. And a lover is a soul of fire! The universe turns differently when Fire loves Water.*[8]

In order for us to understand the truth, we need to allow love and detachment to be the determining

---

[8] Shafak, Elif, *The Forty Rules of Love: a novel of Rúmí,* Penguin Books, 2011.

The Code

factors. To make powerful choices that can have a profound impact on our lives, we must learn to let go of our shadow side, to be detached from the outcome and to allow love to guide our decisions. Think of a recent decision with which you struggled. Would you have made a different choice if you were truly detached and had immense love for yourself and others?

> *A rich man and a poor man lived in the same town. One day the poor man said to the rich man, "I want to go to the Holy Land."*
>
> *The rich man replied, "Very good, I will go also."*
>
> *They started from the town and began their pilgrimage, but night soon fell and the poor man said, "Let us return to our houses to pass the night."*
>
> *The rich man replied, "We have started for the Holy Land and must not return now."*
>
> *The poor man said, "The Holy Land is a long distance to travel on foot. I have a donkey, I will go and fetch it."*
>
> *"What?" replied the rich man, "are you not ashamed? I leave all my possessions to go on this pilgrimage and you wish to return to get your donkey! I have abandoned with joy my whole fortune. Your whole wealth consists of a donkey and you cannot leave it?"*

You see that fortune is not necessarily an impediment. The rich man who is thus detached is nearer to reality.

There are many rich people who are severed and many poor who are not and vice versa.

If we want to upgrade our lives, we need to have clarity about who we are and accept ourselves. To create clarity for yourself, answer these questions:

- What masks am I wearing?
- What do I gain from each mask?
- What are the fears that prevent me from discarding these masks or personas?

The following steps can help you in evaluating and eliminating the masks that interfere with your personal transformation:

- Accept to be vulnerable and authentic.
- Ask yourself, why am I compelled to hide behind this façade? What is missing?
- What can you change about yourself in order to remove the mask?

Mindset Shift

Transforming ourselves starts with shifting our mindsets and evaluating our beliefs. Shift happens only when we stop making excuses and living in the shadows of other people's expectations; rather, we consciously choose our lives and shine a light on the truth.

To restore your passion and make the shift, ask yourself the following, without forcing an answer right away:

- What are my extraordinary gifts beyond life's ordinary circumstances?
- What opportunities are in front of me that will allow me to be in the flow?
- What am I living for that is worth overcoming my moods and negative emotions?
- What am I living for that is worth not allowing the negative energy of others to influence me?
- What is the question I really need to ask myself?

Understanding Triggers

Every situation that triggers our emotion informs us that we are in "that" situation to learn a life lesson; and the situation will repeat until it no longer triggers an emotion within us!

A trigger is an external event that stimulates a negative, emotional response in us. When someone says something to us that we don't like, we may get angry with that person. We get triggered when their behavior, attitude or actions are not what we expect.

There are several things that activate our emotions and cause dissonance and inner unrest. Emotions are natural, so we need to be open to feel them. When a trigger brings out a negative reaction such as anger or pain, it is important to identify the root cause of these feelings. Negative feelings are experiences of the shadow ego that can help us understand ourselves better.

Our emotions—as well as how we manage them—reveal a great deal of information about us. Excessive negative emotions communicate discontentment, low self-esteem, lack of confidence and a lack of surrender to the divine will. Positive emotions on the other hand communicate compassion, confidence, and determination. Emotions in general are good indicators of who we are, and of our state of mind. These feelings arise from either external events or from internal self-dialogues and thoughts. We can make a conscious choice to be objective about them and handle our emotions differently, which would help minimize our negative reactions. We can be sure that external circumstances do not cause our negative experiences; rather, it is our states of mind, our emotional responses, and subsequent behaviors causes the circumstances to affect us.

Our brain correlates triggers with events in the past that hurt us, caused pain, or suppressed us. Most of the time, our reactions are an unconscious response because our sensory memory and sensory experiences correlate this event with an event in the past, sometimes causing an emotional reaction before we even know why we are upset. When this kind of scenario plays out, what it normally indicates is the presence of deep emotional wounds or unresolved issues from a past experience that have not been healed or solved. When we develop an understanding of the reasons for these feelings, we can be more objective when faced with these triggers.

Triggers hurt us; we feel angry, hurt, controlled or

judged. We get triggered because some so-called needs that are important to us are not being met. Some common triggers are:

- Disrespect: when we feel unimportant
- Disregard: when we feel ignored for our contribution
- Deception: when we feel cheated or lied to
- Rejection: when we feel abandoned or pushed away

When we are triggered, there is a sequence of emotions and actions where our negative emotions affect our communications and cause us to make wrong decisions that hurt us and damage our relationships with others, leading to disappointments and regrets.

Here is an example of what happens when we are triggered:

1. Trigger: We are triggered by some external situation.

2. Emotional Response: We experience anger, fear, sadness, anxiety, shame, etc.

3. Self-sabotage: We get frustrated by the repeated patterns and think we are not smart enough to avoid such situations. We further sabotage ourselves by thinking negative thoughts, self-medication, drinking, etc. to try to bury these negative feelings temporarily

4. Energy is drained: We lose momentum, get

fatigued, sad, and suffer, which lowers the levels of endorphins in our brains

5. Communication deteriorates: Our emotions impact our communication. We become critical, judgmental and communicate poorly. We say things out of revenge or anger that can hurt our relationships.

6. Decisions deteriorate: We make hasty decisions based on revenge, fear or anger.

7. Power is imbalanced: Our reaction creates a power imbalance between others and us, creating resentments and negative feelings.

As mentioned above, triggers occur when they bring up an old memory of feeling small or weak. For example, perhaps our parents were critical of us when we were children; perhaps they would express disappointment or anger when we didn't get good grades at school or didn't behave a certain way. We, then, would associate anger with not being "good" enough or "smart" enough. Over time, we develop the need for external validation. So, as an adult, when someone disapproves of us, we correlate that with not being "smart" enough or "good" enough and feel the same emotions of loneliness, helplessness, or sadness that we felt as a child.

In most cases, our strong negative emotions are either fear-based or defense responses to situations of the past. To change our response to these emotions, we first need to understand the reasons for the emotions.

When, rather than using the shadow ego, we engage our higher self to recognize a triggering situation, we become more self-compassionate and more objective about the truth of what is really going on. At that point, we can detach from those feelings and make wiser decisions on how to respond.

The following are some practical steps you can take to identify triggers, shift your response mechanism and take appropriate actions. This is how "shift" works: When you declare the cause of the negative emotions, the negative emotions lose their power.

> *When you declare the cause of the negative emotions, the negative emotions lose their power.*

1. Reflect

    a) Identify the most common triggers that cause an emotional response in you. These triggers are often what you want from others. i.e: respect, attention, acceptance, predictability, independence, being understood, being liked, being valued, etc.

    b) Identify your emotional reactions to each trigger. Write down the trigger, the emotions that arise, and your physical reactions.

2. Inquire

    a) Determine the root cause of why you are triggered by asking the following questions:

    - Why are these triggers causing these emotions?
    - Am I really not getting my needs met?
    - What am I projecting to others?

    b) Was there an event in your childhood that could have contributed to these triggers?

    c) Determine behaviors and habits that you have formed as a result of these triggers.

3. Shift

    a) Shift your emotional response by focusing on what you need instead of what you want!

    b) Shift your emotional response consciously

by focusing on what you want to feel instead of what you are currently feeling, hence changing the habit that contributes to the trigger.

4. Action

   a) List actions you need to take to change behavior traits or habits that you have formed as a result.

   b) What are the opportunities that can benefit from your new understanding of the root cause of your triggers.

Over time, the intensity of the emotions that you experience due to triggers will be reduced; and eventually you will be able to eliminate them or quickly recover from them. As you learn to see the truth beyond the triggers, your capacity for self-compassion and self-love expands.

CHAPTER 9
SIX TYPES OF DESIRE

Understanding Desires

The starting point of all achievement is desire. Not a hope, not a wish, but a keen pulsating desire which transcends everything. — Napoleon Hill

Poets have always characterized desire as their longing for ultimate joy. Some see it as a feeling we have that encourages us to pursue our goals. It can even be considered as fuel for the passion required for any kind of transformation.

> *Everyone has been made for some particular work, and the desire for that work has been put in every heart. — Rúmí*

Desire, as we are using the term, is a longing that flows from deep-rooted knowing or instinct. This longing causes us to pursue only what is in harmony with our divine purpose. Desire comes from our inner soul, not from ego-driven wants such as personal gain, pleasure, or the avoidance of pain.

Desire is the creative source that, when accessed with purity of motive, can actualize an invisible force, transforming and crystallizing it into a visible form. This desire is rooted in our pure thoughts and motives, and based on our consciousness. As a creative force, it has a wisdom already built-in. It can be the DNA of personal creation.

Desire is a strong emotion; if instigated from the space of higher consciousness, it can fuel endless motivation from within us, allowing us to beat logical odds of accomplishing challenging goals.

It is an innate aspect of every human being—this fuel that ignites the passion for creating great outcomes in our lives. It is a strong feeling of wanting something that we believe will lead to ultimate joy, happiness and fulfillment.

Transformed individuals know exactly what they desire and are able to influence others to believe in themselves and become "big picture" thinkers. The key characteristics of such an influencer are: *trust, passion, positive attitude, and motivation*. The passion created by manifesting our desires can have a great impact on the outcome of our lives. When we are aligned with who we truly are and what we want, people trust our insight and our authenticity. When we are aligned with what our heart truly needs, we are able to motivate others to manifest the passion and drive for what they truly need.

FELORA ZIARI

The desire to create is one of the deepest yearnings of the human soul. — Elder Uchtdorf

Six Types of Desire

Philosophers, physiologists and scientists believe that desires are created in childhood and will always stay within us. Sometimes we activate these desires and sometimes we don't. People desire multiple things for themselves.

I believe that there are six main types of desire that can help us ignite our innate power. We could easily get sidetracked if we tap into these desires seeking only wealth, pleasure, or other selfish outcomes without balancing them with altruistic, selfless desires. When we tap into our desires in order to create greater possibilities in our lives, we experience "being in the flow" and feel we are on the "path of least resistance." By being aligned with our higher purpose, we benefit humanity and we feed our soul. When we are fully immersed in altruistic acts, life unfolds effortlessly; and we experience inner peace.

> *When we tap into our desires, we experience being "in the flow" and feel we are on the path of least resistance.*

The six types of desires are:

- **Autonomy:** It is a force within each of us that creates possibilities based on our free will.

- **Validation:** A reflection that our intentions are aligned with our behaviors and the impact we are causing.

- **Romance:** A unique bond with another human being in which we are being loved, seen, and understood, which causes a deeper knowing of self.

- **Significance:** Making a difference in the lives of others. Being appreciated and acknowledged.

- **Expression:** Expressing the uniqueness of our inner creative power into something powerful and meaningful.

- **Joy:** Connecting our inner self-love, consciousness and passion with the outer world, to celebrate this connection, and experience the Oneness.

As you look objectively at each class of desire, ask yourself the following questions:

What are my desires?

What is the outcome of my desires?
Are they aligned with my higher purpose?

What would be my breakthroughs
if I were aligned with my desires?

The First Desire: Autonomy

Autonomy is a powerful desire. It is the ability to make choices on the basis of our free will. Autonomy exists in each individual. It creates personal power, which is described as a force that can create results. Autonomy can create a meaningful life when free will is used to make conscious choices with consideration for all involved.

The lack of autonomy and personal power creates pain, unhappiness and sorrow. When we are not able to speak up and use free will to express ourselves, we become victims and are hindered from living our full potential.

Most of us are motivated to achieve success, develop a powerful presence and, most importantly, realize our passion and purpose. Personal Power, or the *will to power*—a prominent concept in the philosophy of the German Philosopher Friedrich Nietzsche, is the main driving force in human achievement, success and ambition. Personal power creates the drive that gives us the courage to take action.

Personal responsibility is one of the most important aspects of personal power. Personal responsibility is defined as a person's "response-ability", the willingness and ability of that individual to be accountable for their actions. Personal responsibility depends on one's character and maturity level. *When a responsible person responds to a challenge, they do not blame others for their failures or misfortunes; rather, they accept responsibility for their contribution, or lack thereof, to the situation.*

Our state of mind and our actions should not be based on external motivations nor affected by external causes. With personal responsibility, the outside stimuli do not control our responses; we become the creators of our lives, our choices and our destinies. When we take personal responsibility for our actions, we are mindful that our actions and attitude will result in greater outcomes than if our actions were solely due to external reasons or stimuli.

> *Our state of mind and our actions should not be based on external motivations nor affected by external causes.*

While we lack autonomy and personal power, we are often forced to choose from a limited set of options, none of which are ideal. However, with a healthy state of mind and mindset, we learn that we sometimes need to compromise in order to create balance and harmony. If we use our personal power to make a choice that benefits our collective well-being, this type of conscious compromise adds to our inner peace without causing any resentment. The awareness of how to use our personal power effectively is developed through self-discipline, which motivates us to make informed decisions and to use our free will in a constructive and positive manner for all involved.

There are two ways in which we exert or exercise our personal power. One is Internal and the other is External. When we use personal power by tapping into our higher nature vs. our lower nature, our thoughts, our decisions and our actions will be in harmony and we will be able to let go of the non-essentials such as power struggles, unnecessary expectations, emotional reactions, judgmental attitudes, etc.

Internal Power: The power that is expressed in the form of influence over our thoughts, choices and actions.

Internal power can literally change our lives in an instant if we choose to use it effectively. Our mind is the most powerful tool we have; it can be used to redirect our choices and decisions. We can use our inner power to discern how we want to see the world, how we want to live in it, and how we want to impact it. It also directs and influences our emotional attitudes and our emotional responses.

> *We can use our inner power to discern how we want to see the world, how we want to live in it, and how we want to impact it.*

In order to expand our internal power, we need to first know and understand the reasons behind our motives. What is the driving force or the motivation that is influencing each of our decisions? Internal power is most effective when it is based on mindful decision-making involving deep reflection on our motives.

THE CODE

External Power: The power that is communicated in the form of influence or control over our surroundings or others.

External power can be used to create or to destroy. When this power is used for the right reasons, it separates the game changers from those who are solely trying to survive in the society. Power whose sole purpose is to control others can cause harm and imbalance to everyone involved.

The question to be asked therefore is how can we strengthen our personal power in order to use free will and create positive impacts and influence? This requires us to understand several things: our wants, our purpose and our motives, all of which require us to look at the subtle motivations behind our actions and behaviors, the reasons for any power struggles or imbalances, the shadow side of our wants,

> *We need to act consciously and proactively rather than simply reacting to external motivators.*

and the emotional aspects of our actions. We need to act consciously and proactively rather than simply reacting to external motivators. Most importantly, we are the masters of our choices and not the victims of external conditions.

By being an observer of our thoughts and emotions, we can be more objective as we witness our reactions, and adjust our behaviors accordingly. It is not about judging ourselves in comparison to someone else; rather, it is comparing our thoughts and actions to the standard of our higher self—a person who is consciously manifesting a higher state of existence. If we are to achieve new possibilities, break new barriers, then a regular assessment of, and an upgrading of our behaviors and habits is essential.

In order to realize the desire for autonomy in a way that can benefit you, you need to:

- First, take personal responsibility for your own reality and the truth by building a bridge between your thoughts and your actions. *Express your personal power consciously to the outside world.*

- Second, acknowledge that you are in control of your perceived reality regardless of the outside influence, motivators or circumstances. *Accept that no one can influence your actions or reactions.*

- Third, be firmly rooted in values of integrity, humility and courage when exercising either your internal or external power. *Uphold the highest integrity first with yourself and then with others.*

- Fourth, understand your desire for autonomy; your ability to make choices is based on your own free will. *Reflect on the motives that inspires your actions.*

The Second Desire: Validation

Psychologists believe that human behavior is very complex. They tell us that our behavior is influenced by reward and punishment—that we receive either positive feedback that reinforces behaviors that benefit us, or negative feedback that rejects behaviors that could cause adverse outcomes or emotional turmoil. Reward and punishment work well when we are training a puppy, but as people who are growing in self-mastery, we must go beyond this limited view of human motivation. We need to free ourselves from looking at external feedback as the only guide to improving our performance.

Some people play victim by believing that the external events have compelled them do what they do instead of believing that they are in control of their behavior. As we progress beyond this limited view, we find that the outside world need not control our thoughts or actions; rather, it is the choices that we make in the face of circumstances that drive our behaviors.

We all desire to be relevant, to be effective and to be recognized for our effectiveness. We all want to feel accepted by our friends, family and coworkers. Valid examples of how we choose not to accept ourselves include constantly berating, judging and beating ourselves up. Validation or the need for approval is one of our strongest emotional needs. Why does it matter? One of the main reasons for the need for approval is love. By being validated by others, we feel accepted and loved. We feel secure about ourselves.

With these needs in mind, we carry out actions, perpetrate certain behaviors, which are only attempts in the fulfillment of this desire.

Pause for a moment to visualize what self-acceptance would look like in your life and how it could affect your desire for validation.

> *Imagine transforming that desire into a positive force in your life where your motivations and actions stem from the desire to do the right things for the right reasons. There is a sense of freedom when we don't need validation from others to be motivated—when our actions are naturally aligned with our divine purpose.*

Why would people not accept themselves? It seems rather negative that you wouldn't accept yourself, but non-acceptance is more common than ever before in today's world. In most cases, the reasons for not accepting ourselves, is a lack of self-love and self-compassion. Another reason for not being able to accept ourselves could be when our actions are out of alignment with our inner knowing and desires. For instance, when we know that one of our actions is based solely on personal gain and personal benefit without considerations for others, we know deep down that it could hurt or harm others.

Validation involves the recognition that our thoughts, behaviors, actions, and even emotions, are understood and are having a desired impact. We want others to realize that our actions matter; we are on the right track; our efforts are effective; and we are making a difference. Self-validation is the recognition and acceptance of our own thoughts and behaviors without necessarily wanting others to see or accept us. Our individual purpose is unique and so is the expression of our desires. When our actions are authentic, we don't second-guess ourselves, we don't need the external validation in order to take certain actions or behave a certain way.

While working as a nuclear engineer, I also started a women's non-profit organization. This change in my life's direction grew out of my authentic desire and need to be a part of the solution to the problem of gender inequality. I found self-validation when I saw women being empowered and finding their higher purpose in life. Not only were they succeeding, but their successes also served to validate my alignment with my calling and my higher purpose.

> *As our self-awareness of our internal motivation grows, we become the source of our own validation. We easily recognize when our outcomes are in alignment with our inner knowing and desires.*

Do you know what you desire?

If we want to know the answer to this question, we need to stop looking outside of ourselves to others for answers; instead, we need to listen to our inner knowing. Instead of making general comments about what we lack, we can make clear requests and affirmations. This requires us to look at our needs, wants and desires without external influences.

Once our internal communication is being used to recognize our desires, we will begin to use this agenda with others. Instead of participating in our friends' conversations about whatever is lacking on the surface of their lives, we will redirect their attention to their deeper desires and their untapped powers, creating a circle of intention that is palpable, powerful, and fun-filled. What this does is to imprint a certain knowing in us, that our behavior now has a positive impact. Our intentions will become pure, causing a positive energy that will not diminish when we are around others who would otherwise suck the energy out of us. If we fail to do this—if we surrender to a negative energy circulating in the outer world—we abandon our dreams.

> *As an inspired individual, we will create our reality by not being a victim of the negative demands that the outer world is making. Instead, we will remain true to the directions channeled from our inner world. By fostering our own pure intention, detached from vain imaginings, our actions will be unaffected by external reward, creating the harmony and peace we are seeking.*

Women, in general, are more relational than men and have a greater tendency, and desire, to be part of a community. This desire to belong can be valuable to us when we channel it so that it is aligned with our higher purpose. Women who are exploring their inner knowing while growing in self-mastery need to keep this relational need in mind so that it becomes woven into their goals in an appropriate way.

The Code

During the process of exploration and growth, there is a danger of falling into the trap of conforming to the social protocols that have existed for women during the last ten thousand years. How do we solve this problem? Creating healthy boundaries can help us rise above it and avoid the old patterns of submissive behaviors.

The Third Desire: Romance

The desire for romance, pleasure and sex is a fundamental aspect of our lives. However, the indulgence in pleasure without a connection to some higher purpose has been a source of problems for many people. Human beings are born with the urge to unite. Throughout our lives, we are driven to be part of a group, a community, or some other entity. This need for belonging motivates us to exert considerable effort to create and maintain relationships and work with others, such that, even when a relationship causes us severe stress, we often attempt to create harmony so that we avoid living in solitude.

When we create relationships with others, it presents us with a double bind. We might ask, *How do I meet my basic needs for relationships while maintaining my personal freedom, my Self?* This conflict can be beneficial. One of the most important truths about relationships is that the conflicts within a relationship allows us to learn more about ourselves. When we observe "what comes up for us" while interacting with others, we understand more about our nature, our needs, and our programming.

One of the primal aspects of our nature is the fear of rejection or abandonment, either of which creates feelings of not being worthy and insecurity. These negative feelings can lead to disengagement and withdrawal from a relationship. When we don't understand these fears, we might overlay the tensions of our relationship with situations that are not related.

For example, a women may react strongly when someone raises their voice and may accept responsibility for their anger because while growing up her father was emotionally abusive towards her mother; and her mother accepted the blame for his anger. Without discernment, she may "take it personally" instead of evaluating the validity of the situation and accepting it as an opportunity for personal growth.

In a romantic relationship, we are creating a deeper bond. We are willing to expose our inner self to another. If we allow this type of connection to unfold mindfully, it will help us delve into ourselves and gain a deeper personal understanding. An imbalance of power exists in the majority of relationships because of the difference in education, knowledge, capacity, wisdom, maturity and enlightenment of the individuals. However, we can benefit from this imbalance if we use the differences as an impetus for developing ourselves and raising our level of self-mastery.

Romantic connections act as mirrors that reflect our true nature. To find where we are in our spiritual development, we need to use our relationship as a compass to find *True North*, our present direction toward self-mastery. Instead of looking into this reflection of our relationship, searching frantically for what we want to see, we can

> *To find where we are in our spiritual development, we need to use our relationship as a compass.*

observe what is actually being shown. This practice can trigger emotions that are charged, either due to our past history, programming about what relationships are supposed to look like, or attachments about the future.

The only way to have a deeper knowing of ourselves is to be open to examine all the scars, charges, and resistance that show up in our relationships.

As an enlightened individual, we will see our romance as a stepping-stone that creates a closer bond with our partner rather than an indulgence that serves as a temporary fix for our unresolved emotional issues.

The Fourth Desire: Significance

Most of us get a sense of fulfillment and satisfaction when we get approval and consent from others. Positive feedback that is channeled back to us for our work can be very fulfilling, whether that feedback takes the form of gratitude, admiration, or monetization. Therefore, we may feel and act differently when we know our accomplishments are going to be acknowledged and that they are meaningful.

Relating to other people is an innate aspect of our psyche. The combination of biology and social consciousness determines the way we act around others. However, making a difference, and improving the lives of those around us, stimulates a greater satisfaction when it is rooted in selfless generosity and noble acts of goodness without consideration for ensuing rewards. The personal satisfaction of helping others comes, not only from our innate goodness, but also from the fact that when we are of service to others, our attention is not placed on ourselves. What a relief! The experience of being of service produces a happiness and joy that expands beyond our own self-interest and into a cause. When our thoughts and our innate desires are in harmony, our actions create a much greater impact.

> *Most of us get a sense of fulfillment and satisfaction when we get approval and consent from others.*

FELORA ZIARI

I slept and dreamt that life was joy.
I awoke and saw that life was service.
I acted and behold, service was joy.
—Rabindranath Tagore

If you ask a bunch of four year olds still in a state of curiosity, "What would you like to do when you grow up?" they almost always list roles that serve humanity, whether real (a nurse, fireman, or astronaut) or fictional (Batman). Maybe that childish desire to be of service can be part of our adult vision. We live in a world in which we can have physical abundance while being a great contributor to the well-being of others.

Being of service, or giving back, can be a source of willpower. It allows us to go beyond our personal self-interest and avoid the emotional conflict between success and humility.

> *Service which is rendered without joy helps neither the servant nor the served. But all other pleasures and possessions pale into nothingness before service which is rendered in a spirit of joy.*
> —Mahatma Gandhi

Two things take place in our brain that affect the outcome of our action when we are in service to others.

1. The first point relates to interconnectedness of our thoughts and our actions. Our brain is made up of nerve cells. These nerve cells interact with each other and create an electric field. This electric field has an energy that can be easily measured. Our thoughts, which are

formed in our brain, are electrical impulses created in this electric field and therefore have energy. The energy of our thoughts has a direct correlation with our actions. For example a positive thought of helping others possesses much higher energy than a negative, hurtful thought. The energy of this positive thought creates a more powerful outcome when compared to a negative low energy thought, which makes us feel good about our choices.

2. The second factor relates to the interconnectedness of our action and joy. Neuroscience has confirmed that when we are being of service to others, or donating to a good cause, our level of happiness is elevated and we feel good about ourselves. When we are happy, our brain creates more serotonin, oxytocin and dopamine. These neurochemicals boost our mood, our overall physical health, and consequently we relax, become more joyful and then we become more empathetic towards others. This feeling of happiness then makes us want to give some more.

The power of our thoughts and the joy created by selfless actions elevate our lives. When we are outwardly focused on the good of others while taking care of ourselves, our thoughts, our inner desires and our actions are all in harmony. We act consciously from a place of abundance, love and generosity. We become a magnet that attracts more abundance, love and generosity. We also attract like-minded individuals into our circle of influence and inspiration, individuals who can help us further our goals and desires.

> *This is the magic: when our thoughts, our attitude and our behavior are adjusted so they are in sync with what we want, then the internal and external vibrational energy of our thoughts and the result we are looking for are linked and we are able to attract the outcome we desire.*

> *I don't know what your destiny will be, but one thing I do know: the only ones among you who will be really happy are those who have sought and found how to serve.*
> —Albert Schweitzer

The Fifth Desire: Expression

We are innately unique beings who often get caught up in judgments of ourselves as well as of others. We can become brilliantly creative when we are open to viewing the world with new eyes—untainted, and without judgment about what it was or how it should be. The power of discernment gives us a clarity that allows us to be in alignment in every situation. This puts us in the state where an "effortless stream" of expression leads to a state of infinite and unique creativity, a state that is very contagious and inspires others to step up and do the same for themselves. The expression of our creativity manifests itself when we are excited about new possibilities and, rather than conforming to the "norm," we are aligned with our natural gifts, disposition and wisdom.

> *Creativity and the "norm" are mutually exclusive.*

Conversely, if we try to conform to our perceived tribal goals, our uniqueness fades away. When we resist our true nature, we are not aligned with the goals that derive from our inner knowing.

Creativity and the "norm" are mutually exclusive. If we are following the norm, by definition, we are doing something that has been done before. We are duplicating, not creating. When we are creative, we are making something new—something completely outside the norm.

We are continuously either creating something out of nothing or creating something out of something else. When we are in the flow, our desires are manifested effortlessly.

> *Some men see things as they are and ask why.*
> *Others dream things that never were*
> *and ask why not.*
> *—George Bernard Shaw*

The creative expression of the inner wisdom and the inner knowing that we each uniquely hold within us is manifested in order to either heal our wounds, or to bring out our deepest desires and to transform them into love and joy. When this connection is made and we feel love and joy as an outcome, we are in the flow of our desires. Sir Ken Robinson, describes this experience as:

> *The arts address the idea of aesthetic experience. An aesthetic experience is one in which the senses are operating at their peak, when we are present in the current moment, when we are resonating with the excitement of this thing that you are experiencing, when you are fully alive.*

To truly experience our creative desires, we need to let go of the "shoulds" and the "norms" of our history and our social or cultural standards so that we can connect with a larger field of consciousness that has no bounds or limits. What holds anyone back is viewing the world through the narrow lens of tribal norms—the habits of thinking and action that derive from the small circle of familiar social groups. If we expose ourselves to new experiences, we can create a broader worldview, perhaps an entirely different view. For example, if we were around musicians, painters and artists, our outlook would be different—we would be connecting the dots and closing the gap differently—than if we were born to a blue-collar or a farming family that did physical work. In the same way, if we grew up in a family of classical musicians, we might be constrained by the musical standards of our family, but if we spend a summer on a farm, we may find new musical avenues to explore. In other words, our minds, when stretched, are capable of expanding beyond self-imposed or environmentally imposed limits.

The mind that is stretched by a new experience can never go back to its old dimensions.
— Oliver Wendell Holmes, Jr.

FELORA ZIARI

The Sixth Desire: Joy

Joy is a natural state in which we are aligned with all that is, with no judgment, making all of us a part of a profound solution in the world. It is our very joy that uplifts life. Joy is the path of least resistance.

Childlike joy is experiencing the present moment. Children are elated by simple pleasures since they are uninhibited and not tied to the past or the future. They fully experience everything, even something as mundane as standing on a bridge looking at the passing cars. Even such a simple act could bring joy to adults if we were able to switch off our mind chatter that complains about the waste of time, thus allowing us to enjoy the colors of the passing cars, the sound each one makes, etc. In most cultures, there is a certain age in which a child's joy gets suppressed, typically around the first grade. A child who is six years old might say, "I LOVE everyone!" and really feel that way. However, getting teased or corrected by protective parents or zealous school officials will quickly shut this down, forcing the child to conform to the cultural standards of cordiality.

> *Joy is a natural state in which we are aligned with all that is, with no judgment, making all of us a part of a profound solution in the world. It is our very joy that uplifts life.*

Joy is a state of being. Experiencing joy comes about when we integrate consciousness into every aspect of our lives. We are able to practice effortless living like flowing water where our joy flows, without any resistance, from the ordinary experiences of life. Bruce Lee, the martial arts legend, told his students, *be like water, shapeless and formless, where there is no effort*. Water, he said, adapts to the path and flows easily. The concept of being like water is used in martial arts teaching where the students are asked to improve themselves and their skills by emulating water.

Joy is different from happiness. Happiness is a short-lived experience that is caused by an external event. As much as we pursue happiness in our lives, what brings us joy naturally is when our thoughts are aligned with our inner desires. This is a more permanent state. Joy connects the outer and inner world as one harmonious experience.

Joy is rooted in trust—trust of self, and trust in the Divine. Faith is the common denominator among joyful individuals.

Everyone has a desire for joy, however, this desire has been mostly suppressed because of life's circumstances and challenges. Bringing joy back into our lives is as easy as drinking water. We can be joyous in the face of calamities because there is no other time like this moment in life. If we look closely, we will realize that the many wonderful things in life outweigh the daunting challenges we are facing.

The Basic Concepts of the Cultivate Unit

The Code

FELORA ZIARI

The Flame

The obscured light of the candle,
can in no wise
impart warmth and delight;

The untuned violin,
cannot follow the rhythm of the music,
and sooth the hearts;

Clouded essence,
veiled core,
unrefined heart,
masks our nobility
obscures our passion
conceals new possibilities;

An awakened heart,
discovers the flame of wisdom
discerns the innate desires
hears the music of inspiration
... to create
... to elevate
... to enhance
Every word
every note
of the journey
to reach the ultimate Destination.

The Code

FELORA ZIARI

UNIT 4
OBSERVE

The Code

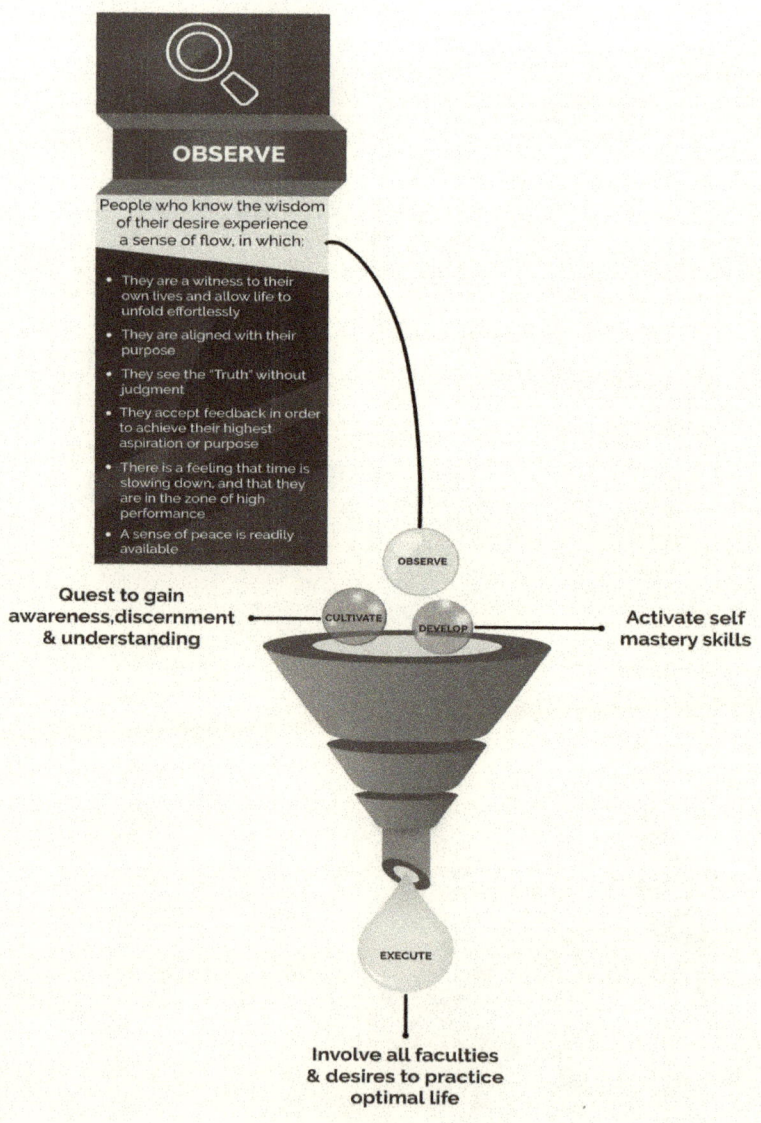

CHAPTER 10
LISTENING TO OUR NEEDS AND DESIRES

Inner Guidance

As mentioned before, the path of transformation begins with the knowledge of self. Without knowledge and wisdom, we may not be able to "see the forest for the trees." Awareness allows us to remove the undergrowth and clear the path to our goals. But without awareness, how do we know what to eliminate, what to add or what to discover?

In this section, we explore the next stage of self-mastery: to pay attention, listen and discover more about ourselves. We either expand by listening to the wisdom of our souls or we shrink by listening to our shadow sides. Our lives will manifest very differently depending on whether we choose to be deluded by our shadow ego or to be guided by our higher self, our soul and the voice of intuition. Meditation is a powerful tool to calm our mind, to find peace, and to mute the layers of noise that can keep us from hearing the voice of our inner guidance.

The mere act of observation and listening can help us recognize where we are and what is important to us. We are then able to address or to redirect our attention and resolve what shows up for us. The following four observations can immediately change our perspective, combat any negativity we are facing and help us move forward:

- What is "Blocking" your happiness? What causes you to be unhappy and prevents you from being content?

- What is "Pulling" on you? What issues or questions are heavy on your mind and pulling you away from your center? What is your negative mind chatter?

- Who is "Hindering" you? Who is affecting your progress and preventing you from achieving your goals?

- Who is "Draining" your energy? Who are the people in your life that drain your energy or impact you emotionally?

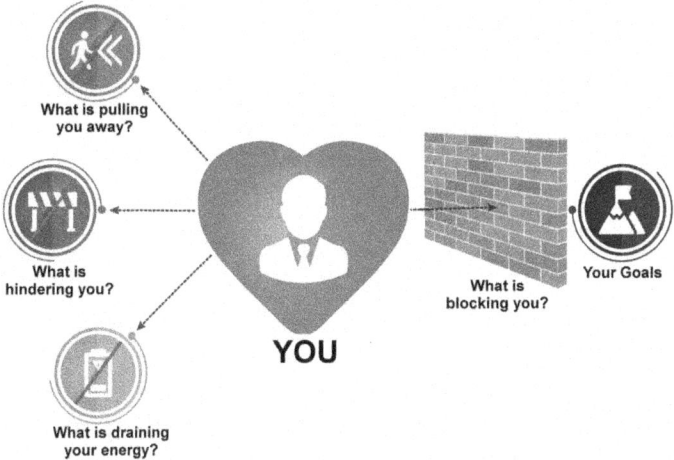

Are Convenient Choices Holding you Back?

Progress seldom comes from acting out of convenience or a sense of obligation. Of course, not all convenient choices are bad or unrealistic. However, much of the time, we make choices and decisions based on what is easy or because we do not want to rock the boat. For example, we may have an old friend who loves to gossip. It will not contribute to our overall happiness if we spend too much time with them out of a sense of obligation. Sometimes, even though our job is not satisfactory, we choose not to do anything about it, preferring to remain unhappy rather than to go through the effort of looking for new opportunities or correcting what is making us unhappy. We cannot excel, or even be happy, when we choose to allow our lives to remain a melodrama. When we make decisions based on convenience rather than on what we truly want, we diminish our inspiration to accomplish what makes us happy. These negative situations are energy drains that consume our thoughts and create imbalance. If we want our actions to be based on conscious decisions, and not simply be driven by perceived obligations, then we need to objectively question our motives. Only then can we be inspired to fulfill the extraordinary lives we deserve.

Once we embrace the choice to live to our fullest potential, we can harmonize with our natural, God-given talents, desires, and yearnings—even if this yearning is simply to do something that makes a difference in the life of someone else. Whatever the case, when we make the choice to open our heart to our desires and let go of negativity, our inspiration will return; and the negativity that is not part of our Divine design will fall away.

After our basic needs are met, and we access the real fire of desire, then we see life through a new lens and become focused, passionate, and accomplished. Suddenly, we can remove the barriers that previously seemed to hold us back. We even begin to be that which we desire, and subsequently attract it consistently into our space. Different methods involving the manifestation of breakthrough outcomes using visualization and affirmation are now widely accessible. However, what's missing from popular methods is the following assertion:

Living up to our human potential requires coherence and alignment between our specific desires, determination, and our actions, all of which are based on our inner knowing, and our values rather than on our cultural programming that was previously pursued blindly.

Curiosity Mindset

Curiosity is one of the significant aspects of the "Observation" part of the CODE. Curiosity can elevate our perception to a new level, leading us to an optimal life. When we are curious, we see the same things that we have seen before; but now it is with new eyes. We learn deeper truths about them. When we are curious, we have an active mind and an openness to discover and to learn. We pay attention to the wonders of the world and are in awe of life and the interactions we experience. We ask "What if ..." questions.

Einstein was a great example. Throughout his life, he constantly questioned everything, the obvious and not so obvious, the familiar or not so familiar. His curiosity resulted in a great deal of innovation.

Curiosity helps us to use the power of observation to learn something new. There are many studies that correlate the curiosity to learn with the enhancement of our daily lives and the creation of joy. Other studies have shown that adults who are more observant and curious have greater analytical ability and success.

One way we can practice the power of curiosity is by being conscious of our surroundings daily. Whenever I am traveling to a new place, I consciously look for clues in my environment to find more information about the culture, the economy and the people. Even when visiting a familiar location, I scan my environment as if it is the first time I am seeing the place. I look for new sounds and smells, trying to get a sense of the place and feel its emotions.

The Curiosity of a Physicist

My dear friend, Professor Asoke Nandi, was part of a team that won the 1984 Nobel Prize for a discovery in physics. I have known Asoke since my college years in England. His wife Marion and I were the only two female engineering students in our graduating class. Asoke is a humble, genuine and very inspiring man. He currently runs the Electronic and Computer Engineering department at Brunel University in England.

One day, I asked him about his perspective on success, knowledge and wisdom and how he came to do what he was doing. Asoke replied, that in life, even as a young man, he never compromised. His professional work and his personal life have always been in harmony. In fact he never looked at his job as work, rather as an extension of his life which he enjoyed doing. He said, "What is better than this? I do my life and I get paid for it."

I asked him about his role models. He said while growing up he read a lot of books, mostly autobiographies that inspired him—not to be like them exactly, but rather to have the same drive for accomplishment. He said that since he was fifteen years old, he knew exactly what he would do and accomplish. He said he knew at that age that he would win a Nobel Prize and eventually be dean of a university.

One thing that Asoke emphasized was that his success was the byproduct of his curiosity about the nature of life. He always wanted to know what it takes to get what you want. He said "Sir Isaac Newton was not the first man that had an apple drop on him, but he was the one that asked why the apple dropped."

It is very important to be curious. Sometimes we think what is familiar is obvious, because it's there, but the deeper answer can be anything but obvious.

Live Fully, See Fully, Feel Fully

We can easily move from regular life—the melodrama projected onto the screen of an average mind—to an amplified and creative life by accepting the call of our desires, but more importantly, honoring that call and putting it in motion. Each of us can probably remember an event that caused us to peek behind the screen to get a glimpse of our true purpose.

In my life, my journey to find my passion and desire began through my conversations with my grandfather. Once, when I was a teenager, my entire family gathered around my grandfather to hear his stories from his recent trip to the United States. It was a day that changed my perception of my future. Grandfather told us stories of his travels and the beauty and modernity of the country. The room was full of people who could not imagine life outside of Iran. He told of how, in the USA, his strongest impression was that the people—even women— had freedom of expression. He told us that Americans are allowed to "live fully, see fully and feel fully." I was awestruck with his descriptions. I asked him later, "How can I manifest a life where I live fully, see fully and feel fully?" My grandfather looked at me, smiled knowingly and said, "Felora, one thing I learned while traveling the world is that everything is possible, and I have no doubt that with your determination and courage you will achieve whatever your heart desires." I have thought about his remarks for a long time.

Through his continual validation of the freedom of expression of all people, he challenged me to embrace my freedom of expression and live my life based on what I wanted, rather than on the demands of others.

My grandfather's validation of "Me" set me free to continually examine the masks that I had put on myself. With his belief in me, I set out to prove that I could achieve my heart's desire. First I became an engineer, a traditionally male role at the time, and worked in the nuclear industry for sixteen years. I soon realized that this so-called "achievement" was not a measure of my value or my true purpose in life.

My true journey began when I remembered my dream as a teenager, which was to live in a world that acknowledged a person's value as a human being—a value that was based on neither gender nor race. I realized that my purpose was to make a difference by being a vehicle to alleviate the gender imbalance, and thus contribute to the advancement of women. My calling was to be a source of inspiration, empowerment and encouragement for a new generation of leaders.

Because of this desire, I founded multiple businesses and nonprofit organizations geared towards transformative, personal self-mastery and professional development for women, encouraging them to break through any limitations that had kept them from stepping into new possibilities.

The Code

CHAPTER 11
TWO PILLARS OF TRUST AND DETACHMENT

What gets in the way of our moving forward?

Our fears, inner judgments and lack of clarity influence our state of mind and impact most of our decisions, hindering our progress and evolution. Trust and detachment are two foundational pillars that can help us overcome the negative voices and apprehensions that we may face. With these two foundational pillars, we are able to surrender by letting go of the control and accepting that there are instances in our lives where we cannot influence the outcome.

Pillar of Trust

> *When the roots are deep,*
> *there is no reason to fear the wind.*
> *— African Proverb*

When we are in the process of applying the CODE

elements of Cultivate and Develop, trust is a very crucial factor for getting better results. Trust is the foundation of every relationship, whether with ourselves or with others. It begins when we accept ourselves, our purpose in life, and others for who they really are. Trust is also about respect. Acceptance alone is not sufficient. We need to respect our choices, our values and our relationships. Any relationship that has as its core the principles of acceptance and respect becomes quickly elevated to a new level that uplifts and inspires all involved.

Trust helps us implement our mission and achieve our goals by letting go of fear and anxiety about things that we don't understand. Trust adds value to every relationship, deal, contract, and operation. It creates influence and impact by eliminating the suspicion and doubt that stem from the fear of the unknown. Trust is the opposite of fear. While fear is mostly about what we want in the future, trust is about the present moment.

It is much easier to have a relationship or interaction with others when we trust them. When we know that others have integrity, high morals and values, we can take action faster and optimize the outcome. We always know whether others are trustworthy because everyone subconsciously sends out signals that we feel in our gut. When people are asked why they trusted someone who they hardly knew, the majority would say, *Because I felt that I could trust them.* Of course, the opposite also happens—that we felt a certain individual couldn't be trusted. Most of the time, we don't know exactly why we trust or mistrust them.

When considering our own actions, we need to realize that others can feel the same way about us. They may not be sure if they can trust us or not. We can earn the trust of others by honoring our commitments and realizing that they will sense if our actions are not authentic. When trust exists between people, there is more assurance about the intentions of all parties. This type of clarity creates a freedom of expression so that everyone involved can devise more innovative solutions to problems.

In one of the largest and most extensive surveys of its kind, Watson Wyatt studied 12,750 U.S. workers in all major industries and work levels to determine the impact of the employees trust in management. According to the study, "Companies with high trust levels generated total returns to shareholders at almost three times that of companies with low levels of trust."

Trusting others may be easier than trusting ourselves. Self-trust is sometimes hard to understand or grasp. Self-trust is a combination of four elements: self-reliance, self-love, self-compassion and self-regard. With these four elements are present, we can trust ourselves and our choices.

I have often been asked: "What does trust look like in your life?" *To me, trust looks like a river. The obstructions of the riverbed ahead are opportunities that either create a beautiful waterfall or another opening. Both of them will lead you to another river or to an ocean. Therefore, trust is an inner state that is not dependent on the impediments rather it flows naturally around them and becomes even more effective.*

When we apply trust to cultivating our core, we create values that are not based on the shadow side of our ego but rather on the wisdom of our desires and our higher self. As mentioned before, Trust is a combination of four elements of self-reliance, self-love, self-compassion and self-regard. When developing and cultivating our core, we need to trust beyond what we know or believe. Trust is based on faith and being able to see the end at the beginning. In other words, we develop the ability to project into the future and visualize what we want to accomplish as though it has been materialized.

Developing skills and changing habits and behaviors requires discipline and awareness. We need to trust our core beliefs and values in order to be guided on a path that is not delusional. When we do not trust ourselves, we self-sabotage; we focus our attention on what is lacking in our lives instead of accepting and being grateful for what we have. We look for others to satisfy the needs or wants that are missing in our lives rather than being self-reliant.

One very important thing I have realized is that in order to sustain the journey of personal development, the four elements of self-reliance, self-love, self-compassion and self-regard have to be integrated into the core of who we are. What follows is a definition of each of these elements:

Self-Reliance is the ability to rely on our own power and exercise our will based on our personal experiences. It is also about taking personal responsibility and making decisions based on wisdom.

> *I am thankful to all those who said NO to me. It's because of them I did it myself. -A. Einstein*

Self-Love is very misunderstood. Self-love is not selfishness. Rather, it refers to understanding and loving all aspects of yourself, the good characteristics and the not-so-good aspects that you are trying to heal, understand or improve. If we don't understand an undeveloped aspect of ourselves that has negative qualities, perhaps rage or anger, we can still love all the other great things about ourselves. But most importantly, we need to love the efforts we are making towards improving ourselves. We need to appreciate those efforts as much as all the good qualities we have. What makes us human is that we are not perfect, however every day we strive to be better than yesterday.

Self-Compassion is the ability to have empathy, consideration, kindness and benevolence towards ourselves. We all know that sometimes we can be harder on ourselves than we are on others—because we know what we expect of ourselves and when we fall short of these expectations, we are distraught. However, how can we truly be loving to others if we cannot be compassionate and kind to ourselves?

Self-Regard is the ultimate respect, reverence and honor for our own selves, our desires, our choices and decisions. When we have self-regard, our choices and our actions will be based on integrity and high moral values. When we have respect for ourselves, we are able to pass on this virtue and show respect to others.

> *I don't trust people who don't love themselves
> and tell me, 'I love you.' ...
> There is an African saying which is:
> Be careful when a naked person offers you a shirt.*
> *— Maya Angelou*

Trust and Doubt

> *What makes a river so restful to people is that it doesn't have any doubt; it is sure to get where it is going, and it doesn't want to go anywhere else.*
> *— Hal Boyle*

Whatever our mind thinks about, our attention will concentrate on. Our attention is like a switch that can be turned on or off, like a spotlight in the dark. When our minds dwell on scarcity and lack, then our attention will be focused on lack; and that will tend to be what we see and experience in our lives—lack, unfulfilled needs, and frustrated desires. However, when we focus our attention on abundance and are grateful for the positive aspects of our lives, then we are able to experience more of that.

When we consciously choose to understand the context of each new decision and identify the truth behind the "why" of the decision, then we are able to make decisions easily and have confidence in our choices. Without self-awareness, our level of trust in our decisions is weakened. Without conscious thinking, we may be unable to prioritize the various parameters of a decision. If we cannot prioritize, then the conflicting parameters will seem equally important, making the decision painful, or even impossible. For instance, if taking a new job means moving to another state where you have no family or friends, you may be unable to decide unless you can decide whether the extra money is more important to you than your relationships, or vice versa. Life is full of these decisions, some small, some life-changing. Whenever a decision appears difficult, it is often because we have failed to prioritize some of the criteria.

As we make our decisions, and afterward proceed to implement the decisions, our thoughts must be in harmony with our actions. The energy of our thoughts transmits either negative or positive pulses to our emotions and to everyone around us. We should ensure that these energy forms support our decisions, not transmit doubt or reject the decision. Otherwise, there will be an internal conflict that causes fear and will make the implementation of our action weak and not sustainable.

The difference between people who live fulfilled lives while listening to their heart's calling and people who are still searching for fulfillment is how the latter allow fear to govern or direct their lives. The enlightened individual realizes that fear is either an illusion that can be weakened or eliminated by the truth, or the fear contains a message that can lead them to a clearer understanding of themselves. Fear is mostly based on what we want in the future and the parameters that we set for ourselves. It can fragment our full potential when it prevents us from moving forward.

Pillar of Detachment

The purpose of life is to realize our highest potential by fully developing and utilizing our attributes in order to achieve our ultimate goals and desires. The true meaning of life becomes more evident when we understand our personality, our attributes, and what we "want." Even more importantly, we must know and embody our values.

Volition is one of the attributes that can move us along this path to realization. It is the willpower or the drive that guides us in the manifestation of our desires. However, in order for the will to manifest—the volition to be effective—we need to understand and embody the attribute of detachment.

Detachment means having freedom from things and allowing nothing to control our lives. It does not mean living like a monk, letting go of everything we own, or ceasing to think independently.

> *Detachment is not that you should own nothing,*
> *but that nothing should own you.*
> *— `Alí ibn abí Talib*

In order for us to understand the concept of detachment, we need to understand its opposite: attachment. Attachment means that our happiness or self-validation is dependent on transitory or material things such as material possessions, power, wealth, respect or status. Whatever we are attached to can control our choices and the outcome of our decisions. For example, our decisions must be based on truth, but without detachment may be based on whether or not we will receive certain privileges. Not everything we want for ourselves is wrong or bad; however, how we go about getting them or maintaining them could be harmful in the overall scheme of things if we don't have the right motivation. Ego-based attachments can become an obstruction, a veil preventing us from seeing the truth for what it is. When we have attachment to "things," then those "things" rule our thoughts, our decisions and our actions, preventing our divine purpose from being fully expressed.

To be detached is to seek the naked truth, to discern reality without being distracted by the transitory things of the world, to desire prosperity and success for all and to practice courage, discernment, and self-regard.

The Code

CHAPTER 12
LISTENING TO INNER KNOWING

As you begin to utilize your innate knowing to manifest your desires, you will not only find peace, harmony and abundance in your own life, but also help to create peace and harmony for those around you. However, sometimes you hear your inner voice loud and clear—and it makes sense at the time—but later, you begin to doubt your understanding of it because your ego-desire has begun to cloud the vision. To follow your inner knowing, your inner compass, your intuition, you need to possess a firm confidence in that original inner voice and guidance and refrain from second-guessing yourself.

Practice the following exercise to develop the skill of listening to your heart:

1. Sit in a comfortable meditative position.
2. Ask yourself a question for which you need an answer or perhaps just some clarity. Write the question in your journal.

3. Now close your eyes and focus your attention on your breathing.

4. Meditate as long as you like.

5. If you can, avoid thinking about the question, just clear your mind and be silent.

6. If any thought comes to your mind, do not resist it; let it be and follow the thought. Avoid judging what shows up. Do not label it.

7. After the meditation, quickly write in your journal by allowing the words to flow from your heart (not from your mind). Don't worry about grammar, spelling or even if the sentences make sense. It does not matter if what you write is not very clear. This process will become easier with practice.

This is a very powerful practice. It helps you be in tune with your heart and strengthens your intuition. In this practice, your rational mind is not controlling the information; rather, you are allowing an opening in your heart so the voice of your inner knowing can be heard. It's exciting because, in reality, you are an observer and not a participant. While engaging in this practice, do not force an answer; rather, allow the inner knowing to emerge. This practice gets easier if you welcome what shows up without clouding it with negative reactions, judgments or assumptions.

Later, as you become more experienced in this practice, you will be able to ask a question from your "intuitive heart" and receive the answers more readily and without much effort.

FELORA ZIARI

The best and most beautiful things in the world cannot be seen nor touched but are felt in the heart.
— Helen Keller

To move forward while avoiding the compromise my friend Asoke warned us against, you need to remember two things:

- Who can you be without the pretense of the masks?
- Who can you be without the influence of the triggers?

In order to see beyond your masks, you may have to force yourself to look a little more closely by being honest with yourself.

Have you ever stared at your image, especially your eyes, in the mirror? It is one of the most powerful things you can do. Sometimes when I am looking into my eyes, I do not recognize myself, especially when I am either emotional or completely disconnected from my emotions. Try it yourself. You can see your pain, feel your fear, and see your joy—just by looking into your own eyes. You can see behind the masks to grasp a deeper understanding of who you are, what you want, and why you want it. You will be able to listen to your "intuitive heart" by observing your eyes while you feel the emotional disconnects in your heart.

Emotions are Mirrors

Emotions play a big part in knowing who we are and who we can become. To really understand ourselves, we need to reflect on how we handle our emotions, and the stories we tell ourselves. Emotions are mirrors that reveal our true selves, our attitude towards life, and where we are heading.

The best tool in understanding our emotions is to observe our reactions to the emotions that arise from life challenges, small or big. We can alter our lives by altering our reactions. We can become stuck if we want new outcomes, but act and react the same way as before. In order to change, we can start by setting boundaries for our behaviors and boundaries for how others relate to us. During each new situation, we observe our feelings and then allow the sensations to pass while observing our reactions as if we are someone else who is watching our reaction without any judgment. Doing so will help us understand the roots of the feelings without being distracted by the immediate issues at hand.

> *People who become skilled at self-mastery learn to observe, evaluate and learn from their reactions.*

When an unexpected challenge or an unfortunate event takes place in our lives, we ascribe a meaning to the event by creating a story. The type of story that forms in our mind depends on our personality, triggers, perception, culture and many other things. If we are pessimistic or negative, we give a tragic meaning to the story; we act as victims of the circumstances. This causes deeper problems by creating anger and resentments, which inevitably creates more drama and complicates our relationships. However, if we look at what happened objectively without ascribing any melodrama to it, we are able to look past the immediate problem and see the life lesson that is being offered to us. We will eventually be grateful for the difficulty or the lessons that the situation presented.

The most difficult part of personal development may be acquiring the ability to see things impartially so we don't take them personally. For example, if we were offended because someone we knew ignored us and we considered this rude behavior, our immediate reaction might be to ignore them as well and to reciprocate their rudeness. However, later we might learn that the person who offended us was having a bad day because a family member had just died and they were grieving the loss of their loved one. Their behavior had nothing to do with us. This situation is very common. We need to realize that other people's behavior is rarely about us; rather, it is about their own personal challenges and issues. When we do not take other people's behavior personally, we can see the situation much more clearly or withhold judgment until we have more facts.

There are several aspects to our mind such as memory, sense perception, logic, etc. There is also a purely spiritual part of the mind. Compassion is an innate aspect of all of us. It can shine a light on situations and create clarity. However, sometimes doubt and fear obscure it and we become indifferent. The Dalai Lama says, "If you want others to be happy, practice compassion. If you want to be happy, practice compassion.

To know our true self, we need a spiritual process that includes: prayer, meditation or perhaps reading spiritual books and contemplating the essence of the messages. However it happens, we must strengthen our spiritual mind and spiritual heart so that they are able to have a positive influence on our logical and emotional aspects.

Any method will work if we apply it daily and diligently so the spiritual mind and heart become stronger and the habit of blame is replaced with the habit of praise—gaining the wisdom to seize the opportunity to learn from everything, and being grateful for each opportunity.

> *When we are clear about the attributes needed to manifest our desires, we will not be resisting those desires; rather, we will be in the flow of our goals*

Growing in self-mastery is a logical process. We must think about what we want and draft a plan to take us there. Part of that plan will involve making conscious choices about our vision, our purpose, our strengths, and areas that we need to improve. With a little self-mastery, we are able to look at ourselves honestly, and compare ourselves to the attributes required to achieve our desires, and then make acquiring those attributes part of our plan for success. In other words, who do we need to become for our outcomes to occur? What attributes are dormant in us that must be expressed or strengthened for our desires to manifest?

More patience? Empathy? Negotiation skills? Laughter? Silence? Fitness? Professionalism? Polish? Softness? Politeness? Spirituality? Discipline?

We are not talking about becoming someone else, although we can look to role models for clues to what we must bring out in an authentic life. When we are clear about the attributes needed to manifest our desires, we will not be resisting our desires; rather, we will be in the flow of our goals. When we are in the flow, we do what we love to do, what lights us up. We experience time differently; it flows easily and joyfully.

The Code

The Basic Concepts of the Observe Unit

The Code

FELORA ZIARI

The Road We Journey

Through the cocoon of darkness
blended web of illusions
veils of misunderstanding
moments of happiness and joy
the road
we journey

Knowledge and perception,
faculty of reflection and discovery
our guide
breaks down the masks
removes the barriers
awakens
deep wisdom
honor
inspired voice
with courage, strength
and
steadfastness

So we can observe
the brilliance of life
the expanded view
the road
we journey.

The Code

FELORA ZIARI

UNIT 5
DEVELOP

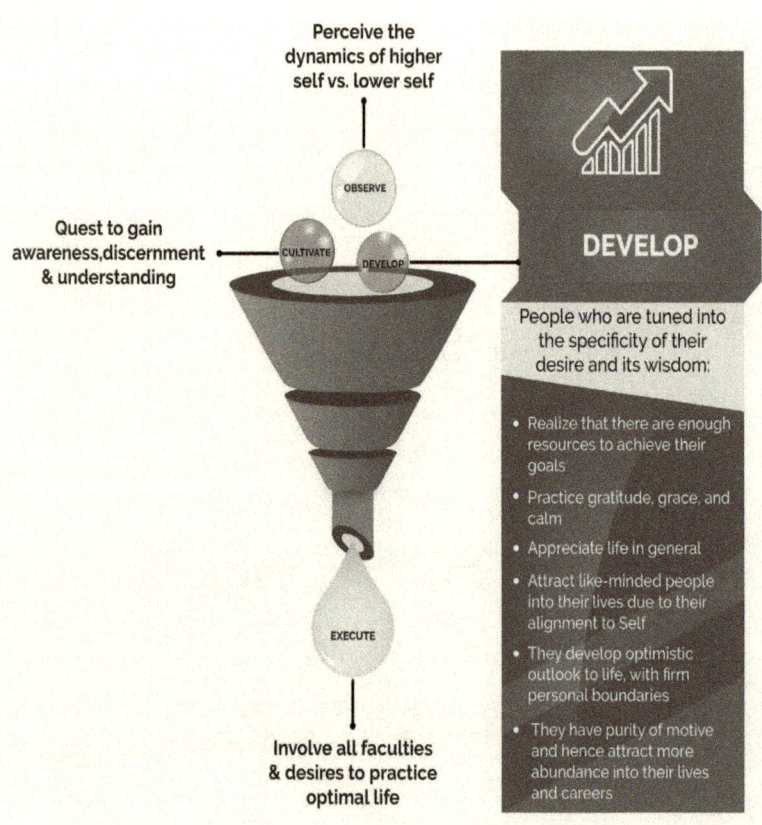

CHAPTER 13
OPTIMISM

Optimism, positive thinking, conscious discernment, and mindfulness are all great skills in personal development. However, if we fail to create the right environment to sustain those skills, we can quickly revert to feeling powerless when it comes to the achievement of our goals. We need to practice these tools regularly so they become habits while creating a new lifestyle infused with optimism and confidence.

Have you ever pondered on why we endeavor to learn certain new skills? Well, if you think about it, the only reason to learn new skills or gain knowledge is to enable us perform better. Without that outcome, the learning is meaningless. Effective performance is the fruit of the tree of knowledge and understanding. However, to have peak performance we also need to be in harmony with ourselves and with our environment by practicing conscious discernment.

The Code

True personal development causes disruption in our lives, in our choices and in our relationships. There is no way to avoid shaking things up. Just reading personal development books will not help us change. We also have to transform our way of being, doing and thinking in order to overcome the challenges of disruption. Furthermore, we must acknowledge that disruptions are necessary to achieve the outcomes we are looking for.

Disappointments arise when the outcome of our efforts does not match our expectation. The funny thing is that we are often disappointed because we fail to take cues from our innate wisdom, we fail to be guided by it and so we get disappointed. Our shadow-ego prevents us from accepting the guidance because of its attachment to a certain outcome.

In this unit, we will explore how we can access the inner energy and the inner power by decluttering the beliefs, relationships, and objects that obstruct peak performance, harmony, and joy.

Imbalance arises from negativity, balance from positivity!

Problems arise from scarcity, solutions from abundance!

Worries arise from lack, joy from acceptance!

So, what really matters? Is it balance, positivity, abundance, acceptance or the opposites? Unconsciously, we make choices all of the time—to be part of a solution or part of a problem.

FELORA ZIARI

Are Your Dreams Big Enough?

I have often asked myself what makes people dream small and be content with those dreams. I have also discovered, over and over again that it is the fear of the unknown and fear of disappointment that makes people dream small. We sometimes prefer to stay stagnant rather than to go through the struggle that change and transformation demands of us. Before we can build a new life, we have to sweep away some, or all, of those old habits, mindsets, and attitudes that were a part of our former life of limitation.

Before we build a new house, we have to clear the land.

The only reason I left my job as an engineering manager to start a non-profit organization for women's empowerment was because of my deep-rooted knowing that, at that point in time, my highest desire was to raise the banner of gender equality and to empower women to follow their dreams. On the surface, it was not a good decision to leave my job. However, my passion for service and social good was palpable. Since then, my life has turned in so many directions that I could not have imagined. Indeed, making the decision to embark on this new journey was the best decision I ever took in my life. I have experienced such personal transformation and worked in so many different fields including: leadership development, global peace building and conflict resolution, women's advocacy, United Nations advocacy, entrepreneurial development, and global outreach. Of course, none of that would have been possible if I stayed in my safe role as an engineer and did not follow my inner desire and passion.

Disintegration is a prelude to integration. It is necessary for our lives to come undone so we can open up to new possibilities.

The following steps can be a useful tool in enhancing and honing your faculties so you are prepared to embark on your journey. Make an agreement with yourself to commit to the challenges that will come up.

1. Meditate on this question: "What do I truly want?"

2. Observe your resistance to your choices or your commitments; "What am I resisting?"

3. Observe yourself regularly to see what ideas or opportunities light you up and create excitement. "What lights me up?"

4. Acknowledge your motives and be honest about the power struggles between you and your shadow-self. "What are my motives?"

5. Make a decision to listen to what comes up for you! Remember choice should be proactive! "What are the new opportunities?"

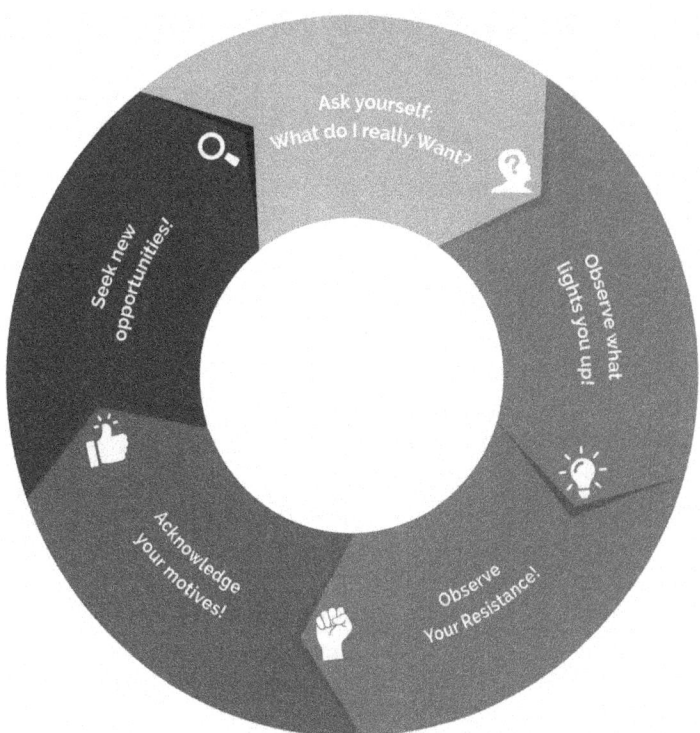

Transformation will only take place when we acknowledge that certain behaviors will hold us back. The shadow side of our ego is like gravity; it persistently brings us down. It is a heavy load that burdens our soul, preventing us from finding our destiny.

Michelangelo famously described how he created his masterpiece sculpture of David, "It was easy; all I had to do was chip away everything that did not look like David." In reality that is how we can perfect the sculpture of our new self—by chipping away what is not needed so the gem of our noble essence can emerge!

The Power of Gratitude

When we are anxious or worried, we put demands on our body that result in an actual energy drain that we can feel. Many people have more frequent illness or pains and aches in their joints as a result. Studies have shown that in order for us to cope with worry and anxiety, our brain releases adrenaline and cortisol into the bloodstream that consequently triggers physical reactions to help our body get ready for action—for a "flight or fight" response to the worry. Subconsciously our body prepares itself with increased alertness—to either run away or to deal with the problem. Much of the problems and health issues people face today are rooted in the stress caused by prolonged worry and not knowing how to deal with it.

However, there is hope; and this hope is found in the power of gratitude. Studies have shown that feelings of gratitude pump blood to the parts of the brain that control eating, drinking and sleeping as well as our ability to cope with stress. If we replace worry with feelings of gratitude, we will have more energy, determination and, most importantly, enthusiasm for life. Gratitude boosts the neurotransmitter serotonin just like Prozac, the antidepressant medication. With gratitude, we see improvements in sleep, decreased depression, increased happiness and even reduced pains and aches.

So, how do we practice gratitude? Gratitude doesn't mean simply churning out words of appreciation; rather, it is recognizing that everything in life is for our benefit; the pleasant events bring joy while the unpleasant events bring spiritual lessons and provide volition to change. It helps to look at our lives as someone else might see them—seeing all that is good: the supportive people in our lives, our health, our family, the so-called blessings. Then to be truly grateful we must go beyond that to examine the events in our past that seemed so negative at the time and identify the benefits that we derived from the pain. So many times the pain pushed us away from a dysfunctional situation or pulled us toward an opportunity that we would otherwise have missed. Having a daily routine that includes a higher level of gratitude has proven to be one of the most effective ways of living a healthier and happier life.

Another benefit of gratitude practice is that we will not feel alone since it will help us see all the connections, all the gifts that life has given us. Through gratitude, we see a forward momentum in our lives. Every day, I start my morning with a practice of prayer and meditation followed by gratitude practice, and then I set three intentions for the day. When I start my day with these practices, I have been able to achieve greater productivity, form deeper relationships and improve my state of well-being. In his book, *Thanks! How the New Science of Gratitude Can Make You Happier*[9], Dr. Robert Emmons, claims that you can

---

9 Emmons, Robert, *Thanks! How the New Science of Gratitude Can Make You Happier*, Houghton Mifflin Harcourt, 2007.

actually increase your happiness levels by about 25 percent by practicing gratitude every day.

Practice the following every day:

- Gratitude Practice: keep a gratitude journal. Be thankful for what is good in your life, compliment yourself for your accomplishments.
- Set three intentions for your day that you would like to achieve.

State of Awe

The more we recognize the limitlessness of universe, the beauty and magnificence of our essence and the power of positive thought, the more we experience Awe and Wonder in our lives!

The practice of gratitude helps us stay present and to remember all that is good in our lives instead of focusing all our attention on challenges and problems. It also reminds us that worrying about the future or regretting our past does not benefit us. Instead it creates fear in us, which causes low vibrational energy, which makes it impossible to receive the gifts of the universe because we are not open to see them. How can we prosper in such a limited state? We can't.

However, we can take the practice of gratitude one step further by being in a state of awe and wonder! When we acquire the mindset of being in AWE of life and all its mysteries and the beauty of our environment and the magical gifts we have been given, then we are able to step into a new paradigm. Our new perspective on life unlocks a creative force by putting us in a higher vibrational energy. Being in awe not only helps us be more joyful and happy, but also helps us be more curious and consequently be more innovative, leading to greater success.

Can you imagine how your work or your life would be transformed if you added the elements of awe and wonder to it? It could be as easy as looking at a rose and admiring the shape, the color, the fragrance of the rose while admiring the majesty of the stem for creating such a magnificent rose! This simple exercise allows us to be present and fill all our time in appreciating every bit of goodness in our lives. Being in awe of the world of mystery—life, creation, and nature—creates a new dimension to our lives; it creates excitement and hope.

> *When we are in Awe of life and its mystery, a magical sense of belonging is created. We are astonished by the beauty that surrounds us! Words become rainbows, transforming the meaning; and our breath scatters our heart's poetry of love far and wide!*

The Code

CHAPTER 14
PURGING THE CLUTTER

What Defines Us?

Roles and positions are other types of masks. We may define ourselves by our achievements rather than who we are as a person. When I left my position as an engineering manager, I realized that when people asked me what I do, I would respond, "I just resigned my job as an engineering manager." However, every time I responded that way, I felt less and less authentic, because I felt like I was trying to prove my worth by what my position had been. In fact, that is what I had been doing for so long! I had to learn to accept myself for who I was at that moment, and what I was doing, without qualifying my worth to anyone. It was a powerful experience to grasp who I was without my former title or achievements.

Now that I could no longer refer to myself as an engineering manager, I had to discover who I was as a person. Who was I, really? I was still a wife, a mother, a sister and a daughter, but those were my roles and not who I was inside. I asked myself, *What are my qualities and attributes as a human being? For what reasons would I love and respect myself as a person!* Once I no longer had an impressive title, I realized that I cared way too much about what others thought of me. I had to find out, *What do I think of me?* Huge revelation! *Who am I—really—without that external role to validate me?*

I learned to examine myself as a human being without the masks, without the roles, and without attachment to being validated by others. Wow! What freedom! I found out that I love to explore and learn new things, to care for others and make a difference in their lives, to laugh and enjoy life. You see, there is so much freedom in knowing yourself as a human being and not your wealth, your title, or your ancestors.

Redefining Ourselves

The first step in the process of decluttering and letting go of what no longer serves our higher purpose is to get some clarity about who we are. Once we begin to assess who we are, we could decide to accept the status quo, or we could decide to move forward by honoring our commitment to self-mastery. We begin by removing the masks that have defined us. This is not an easy step; it requires recognizing and correcting the layers of self-denial that are rooted in fear. And yes, clarity requires considerable discipline. We are mistaken if we think we won't have to fight for it. There will be a battle as the shadow-self tries to hold onto the past.

The second step in redefining ourselves is to commit to the process. We need to make a commitment, a personal agreement that we are willing to make all the necessary efforts to accomplish whatever is needed in order to complete this process.

In my practice of helping professionals along their success journey, I have noticed that when they make a commitment statement to follow through with the process of transformation or achieving a certain goal, they have a much higher chance of accomplishing their goals. We will talk more about the commitment exercise later. However at this point, let's make a short commitment statement to acknowledge that we are dedicated to our journey and will not allow self-doubt or ego to prevent us from moving forward.

Let's be True to ourselves

Human beings have always pretended to be someone other than their true selves. We seem to all have a persona for people we know, a persona for strangers, a persona for people we want to impress, a persona for our children, and a persona for our lover. We show up differently depending on what we want to gain and what is at stake. We also have a private persona that we do not share with others. Each persona or mask takes its toll on us. Getting rid of the deceptive masks does not mean that we will become inappropriately rigid as we interact with various people. Of course we behave one way with our children and quite another in an important business meeting, but in every case, we will be authentic and will not pretend to be someone we are not.

When we routinely present a false persona to others, life becomes very stressful. We will start to have self-doubts because we will be confused about who we truly are. On some level, we know that it is a lie—that we are wearing a mask that is presenting an image to the world that is better than the person we feel inside. Sometimes to our conscious mind, the pretense can seem real; however deep down, we know that we are presenting a façade. We become conflicted and afraid that others might discover our true selves, our shortcomings and our lack of confidence. In our fear, we may blame others for our problems. This phenomenon is very common.

To move beyond these pretenses we need to realize that our biggest fear is this:

If people find out who I truly am, they will not like me!

What if I tell you that most of the people who you truly like and respect are the people who are authentic and accept themselves for who they are—people who do not hide their good or bad personality traits behind a mask? If we truly want a better future, and a better world, we need to show our vulnerabilities and learn to accept them as we work on overcoming them. When we let go of pretenses, our inner and outer worlds are in harmony, allowing us to manifest what we desire. Self-respect and self-love are the byproducts of living authentically and being honest with ourselves. In this process our character becomes more refined and our unique attributes become more visible. Eventually we are able to reveal more self-

On the surface, it seems simple enough to strip away the pretense and just be our natural self. However, the truth is that we all began employing masks at an early age and may have lost all sense of who we truly are. To uncover our natural selves, we need to take a careful look at our core values. One way in which we can effectively achieve this is by a careful analysis of our platforms.

> *When we let go of pretenses, our inner and outer worlds are in harmony, allowing us to manifest what we desire.*

Determining Your Platform

To have a well-lived life, we must have a platform from which we can contribute to the well-being of others. Your platform is a foundation composed of who you are and what you stand for. When that platform is based on your higher purpose and your values, then your work impacts lives and brings hope. Dr. Martin Luther King's platform was to raise awareness on racism, to end racial discrimination and bring about equal rights and social justice in United States. Every historical person you admire must have had some core principles that informed the many decisions they made through their lives that led to an outstanding outcome. Our core principles combined with our desires can create a platform or foundation that can generate our greatest outcome. Based on our platform, we won't be in love with a façade, we will be in love with our true selves.

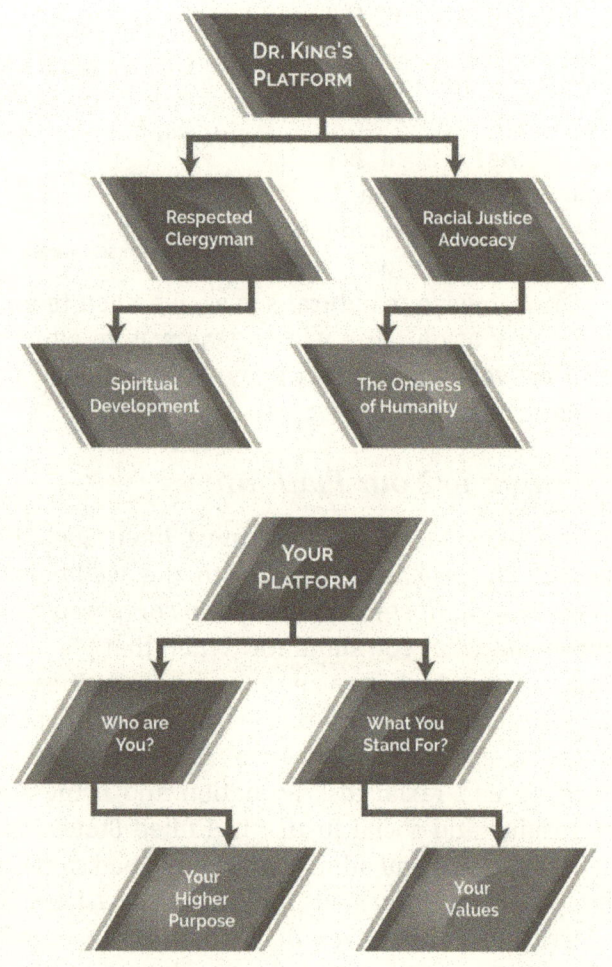

CHAPTER 15
REPLACING BARRIERS AND SELF-LIMITING BELIEFS

Then the question becomes, "What is stopping me from living a life that is aligned with who I truly am?"

Why does success not come naturally, and why are few people achieving it? People have a tendency to resist who they are, hiding their true nature and failing to provide their unique contribution, often for fear of being put out of their tribe.

One thing that blocks us from living our dreams is the tendency to focus on things that are wrong. People who immigrate from countries that are struggling economically to a land of opportunity often have no trouble creating success because they are not caught up in what is wrong in their new environment. When our culture collectively takes something for granted, we lose our real curiosity about that thing. When we lose our curiosity, we lose our passion. When we lose passion, we get depression, escapism, addiction, and entitlement as our results.

Replace Complaining with Gratitude

People have become accustomed to complaining, either about themselves or about others. It has become so normal that we may not hear it anymore. Most people do not realize how much they complain: *The light is too dim or it's too bright; the room is too hot or too cold; it's too noisy; he doesn't hear me; I don't like this or that!* Some people think that complaining is a good way to communicate, to show common interest or to establish rapport with another person. Some of that behavior is learned. We may have seen our parents complain and receive attention from others, so we learned to do the same thing.

> *Complaining is often rooted in an unsatisfied or unrecognized desire.*

The main reason we complain is to satisfy some type of yearning or longing to be noticed or validated. Nothing can cause us to be dissatisfied unless we allow it. Since our reaction to any stimulus is always a choice, we can choose to be either satisfied or dissatisfied.

> *Nothing can cause us to be dissatisfied unless we allow it.*

How we choose to deal with other people's behavior is not dependent on their behavior; it's determined by our attitude.

An average individual complains approximately 15-30 times per day! Of course, sometimes we complain out of a legitimate need for justice or to get our cable TV working again. However, most complaints are done because we fail to take personal responsibility and want to blame others for each negative result. For example, we forget to do something we promised we would do, and then we complain that, *if I had more time or if you hadn't interrupted me or if the rain hadn't distracted me, ... then I would have been able to do what you asked me to do.*

In many cases we complain because we think we know better than others. That attitude can come across as a form of superiority. Whatever the case might be, complaining not only affects us, it affects the other person's image of us. It drains our energy and the energy of the person to whom we are complaining.

People who habitually complain are less likely to take actions and achieve their goals. The reason for this is because negative thoughts create negative patterns that impede the outcome we are seeking. People who complain focus on missing resources instead of focusing on possibilities and solutions.

Studies have shown that complaining, just like worrying, not only causes unhappiness, it actually suppresses the immune system, creating anxiety and many health issues. When we are complaining, we are reinforcing negative thoughts that attract negative things into our lives. To change this pattern, we need to replace complaining thoughts with thoughts of gratitude.

THE CODE

*Ordinary life is transformed to
an extraordinary life when you are grateful for
the "Nobility within you,"
the "Blessings given to you,"
and the "Love shown to you."*

CHAPTER 16
STATE OF GRACE

Are We Attracted to Our Desires?

To be attracted to our desires, we need to be internally motivated—by our interests, curiosity and our core values. These motivations can fuel our passion, creativity and sustained efforts.

Every action, every success, starts with a desire for transformation, change or progress! The problem for many of us is that the creative expression of our desire was crushed by either self-imposed limitations or our interpretation of life's events. Rather than enabling our desire to manifest into something that protects us and serves us, we squash it. When our planet is able to access a fraction of the thousands of creative ideas that are currently being squashed, everyone will enjoy a more productive and ethical planet. Let us work together to bring that which is within us—all those loving, constructive, even great ideas—into the world.

How do we stay motivated? Are we motivated by external rewards, money or praise, or by the internal rewards of passion, values and curiosity? Research shows that we are certainly motivated by both external rewards and internal rewards. The interaction between extrinsic motivation and intrinsic motivation is defined by Self-Determination Theory (SDT)[10]. SDT is a theory of motivation and personality that addresses three innate psychological needs: competence, autonomy, and psychological relatedness. SDT says that if these three needs are met, then we are apt to be motivated and actualize our innate potential.

Competence: The need to control the outcomes and experience mastery of any given situation or tasks to feel competent.

Autonomy: The need to be self-sufficient and act in harmony with the self and be in control of our own goals.

Relatedness: The need for a sense of belonging to a group—for interactions, relationships, connections, and caring for others.

Competence, relatedness and autonomy combine to make us feel good about what we are doing. Removing any one of them will reduce our motivation, so they are necessary—but are they sufficient to maintain our motivation? Even if all three are present, we could be doing something that is ego-centered and not fulfilling

---

10 Ryan, Richard M. & Deci, Edward L; *Intrinsic and Extrinsic Motivations: Classic Definitions and New Directions*; Contemporary Educational Psychology 25, p. 54–67, (2000).

our true purpose. Throughout our growth in self-mastery, we need to continually realign our actions to our higher purpose, especially when our shadow-self starts to lead us astray.

Is This Real, or Just a Movie?

What we experience in life is often a projection of our stories, almost like a movie projected on a blank screen. If we believe we are unloved, incompetent, or a victim, we project those stories on the screen and experience the distortion as if it were real life. If we are projecting misery onto the screen of our mind, then when we have a positive experience, a better job offer or a kind comment from a stranger, we might reject the experience because it does not seem to belong in the sad movie of our life. Sometimes we are so enmeshed in our melodrama, remaining so busy fixing the problems of everyone around us that we forget to pay attention to our own needs and desires.

What we experience in life depends on the extend of our progress:

- We may be successfully attracting our goals directly
- We may simply be enjoying the play of the universe as it moves us through life
- Or we may be living a life of chaos in which we respond to external forces, becoming a victim of circumstances over and over.

Part of self-mastery is being clear about our own desires, clear about the false information in the melodrama we have been projecting onto our mind, and clear about any dysfunction in our relationships. We must continuously reinforce what is true and get rid of what is false. Making ourselves attractive to our desires is similar to caring for a tree. For a tree to bear fruit, pruning is needed. To be successful, happy, and content, we need to prune certain aspects from us. That pruning requires honesty, conviction, honor, and respect for ourselves and the process.

Which of your aspects needs pruning?

Walking a spiritual path

Imagine we are walking a long distance, perhaps across the country. We would expect that certain portions of the path would be smooth and certain portions would be rough or hilly. Some days would be pleasant and warm; some days it would be cold and rainy. If our goal is important enough, we will be happy and look forward to be progressing toward our goal. We might be a little less happy on the cold days, but we will press on, confident of attaining the goal eventually.

Because we are making progress, with each step we must abandon our previous location. Visualize making a step forward: one foot is placed in front of you while the other foot stays on the ground behind you. Can you leave it there? No. That hind foot has to move forward to become the foot in front of us. No matter how pleasant that last step was, we have to move on.

This analogy may seem simplistic at first, but think about your life, about the spiritual changes that are involved as you move toward your goals. Have you fallen in love or become comfortable with some aspect of your life that you hold onto even though it is keeping you from progressing? Is there a belief or an idea about you that is limiting you, keeping you from achieving your destiny? Is that idea like a hind foot that you refuse to reposition in front of you?

These limiting ideas are like some comfortable spot that you find in your travels, a beautiful, flower-filled meadow or a cool creek where you can soothe your tired feet. On your spiritual path, you cannot get too comfortable, you have to press on because something better is waiting to be unfolded, something that you cannot see if you stay in your comfort zone.

Another aspect of this analogy involves joy. If you focus on your goal and on the progress you are making toward it, then you will be happy. However, if your focus is on the hardships of the journey—the muddy section that you are slogging through, or this hill that you cannot seem to reach the top of—then you will be unhappy. If you are beating yourself up because you have not yet attained the goal, then you will not be happy either.

With our goal in mind, we celebrate our progress, and then put one foot in front of the other. Focusing on the joy of achieving our goals can make the process and the journey much easier.

Maintaining a Clear Vision

To master our living legacy and to alleviate negative impacts in our lives, we need to make conscious choices to be leaders—to lead ourselves to reach our destinies by improving each step and each choice made along the way. We need to understand the fabric of our nature and then nurture ourselves to discover the deeper meaning of our lives. In this journey of self-discovery, we are on a quest to overcome and conquer—to overcome barriers and to conquer fears and doubt.

Mastering the Self comes from having deep desires for personal well-being, enlightenment, and peace of mind. Having a vision of a new life that we consciously choose is the first step toward satisfying these desires. This crystal clear vision, combined with the volition to acquire the requisite knowledge and attributes that our vision demands of us, will create a craving for an enlightened self-interest. The love for our personal transformation then becomes so strong and powerful that every word we read, any topic we listen to, and every enlightened individual who crosses our path becomes a teacher guiding us to achieve our goals. Simultaneously, we must make a commitment to stay on the path. It takes disciplined willpower to stay committed.

Setting Boundaries

In truly healthy relationships, there are strong but semipermeable boundaries through which each party gives and receives love and support while allowing each partner to flourish and self-actualize on their individual path. There is a sense of respect and appreciation that allows the other person to live a full life and to explore their own personal potential. If we can establish and maintain healthy boundaries as we live our lives, our trust and belief in this process will grow and mature.

Respecting the boundaries of others is sometimes difficult, especially with our children or with people that work for us. When we feel *overly* responsible for another person's life experiences, we deprive them of one of the most important features of an independent, healthy and mature life: the ability to make their own life choices and accept the consequences of their decisions. Again, this can get tricky. Even people who have stellar, functioning relationships might have an example or two in their lives in which they "let someone make their own choice" even though that choice was an assault on their personal boundaries.

Boundaries can be fragile as long as we are not vigilant. People have an enormous capacity to overvalue the status quo. We may tolerate things in ever-increasing amounts, clinging to the belief that things are "good enough" even though we do not experience all the joy available to us. While living a small, constricted life that feels safe in its familiarity, we rationalize that this is as good as it ever needs to be. In the process, we give up our chance to explore fulfillment, inspiration, and bliss.

We may live a constricted life because of the fear of

damaging our relationships and our so-called security. These fears place limits on us as well as on the lives of others. The antidote is to learn what lights us up and create our lives around that. It sounds simple, but it is often difficult to discover that primary passion. If you aren't sure where your passion lies, observe what makes others come alive. What is it that opens their heart, makes their eyes light up, or causes them to gasp in delight? Could that light you up? Follow this light, and stay on topic in conversations about it. Observe the questions that surface in your mind as you think about the topic. Turn away from any drama. Does it make you come alive? Does it open your heart?

Healthy boundaries allow us to say to others, "I trust and respect you to make your own life choices. We are equals."

How do you apply this?

- First, you have to have a clear vision of what you want. Look beyond your fear of the unknown.
- Why do you have these desires?
- Do you have any unresolved anxieties about your desires?
- How can you transform these anxieties?
- What goes through your mind as you ponder these anxieties? Are you focused on your internal desires or on external motivators?
- Do you have the purity of motive needed to achieve the desired result?

FELORA ZIARI

Visualize the Successful You

History—and most of popular culture—has been defined by men who believed in a competitive, dog-eat-dog, survival-of-the-fittest world. In light of the new age of enlightenment, we must rethink the roles of individuals, organizations and communities in light of the new age of enlightenment, an age that will be increasingly more cooperative and community-oriented. The coming world culture will focus less on benefiting the individual and more on benefiting the community, the nation and the planet. Each of us, women and men, must rethink our personal roles in light of the new reality. Women—the previously ignored half of humanity—must have a vastly expanded role if the new reality for all humanity is to be more balanced, peaceful and prosperous.

We are still learning what a successful woman looks like, and acts like, in different environments. Our collective desire for gender equity will not be fulfilled until we examine the male-generated opinions that we have inherited, discard the ones that do not serve us, and replace them with visions of success that come from a heartfelt approach. Women need to define themselves based on their own criteria and find role models, male or female, who show us that it is OK to just "be ourselves."

> *Desire must generate a strategy that leads to a life of fulfillment rather than a force to achieve a success that is based on criteria defined by others.*

The Code

Desire must generate a strategy that leads to a life of fulfillment rather than a force to achieve a success that is based on criteria defined by others.

CHAPTER 17
GAINING CLARITY

Identifying what you want can clearly help you to manifest your goals and attract them into your life. Clarity will begin to create the situation that allows your desires to be manifested. Your inner resources are infinite, what you need is to trust and take action.

> *Ultimately, we must learn to trust our self. When we do this intimately and intelligently, the world opens full of meaning before us. We find that we ourselves are the doorway to a fathomless understanding of the source of life itself. We need only to learn to walk through it.*
> —*James Thornton*

In order to acquire the necessary attributes, we need to love who we are, be attracted to our values and uniqueness, and respect ourselves. This requires the ability to understand our present characteristics, accept who we are, and then transform aspects of ourselves that does not fit the vision of the lives we are seeking. We will become increasingly conscious of our thoughts, emotions, and behavior. Self-Mastery is not about artificially controlling or limiting ourselves; rather, it is about removing limits and uncovering our hidden skills and desires so they can blossom, benefiting us as well as others.

The following are some steps that can help you in self-examination:

1. Learn from each experience through examining your emotions and how you manage them.
2. Watch how you react to a negative comment. How does it makes you feel? Do not take things personally. It is rarely about you.
3. Observe your thoughts as if you were an outsider looking in. Replace negative thoughts and self-talk with positive thoughts.
4. Understand different personality types. Do not get offended if others act or react differently than you. Remember, it is not about YOU! For example, an analytical person talks in numbers, which can be frustrating if you have an expressive personality or vice versa. A boisterous person may be offensive to a quiet, introverted person. Develop a sense of humor about the diversity in human personalities.
5. Guard against your own negative reactions. Transform your negativity into gratitude by looking for the life lesson in every event. You can change a negative attitude and response by

being a "witness" to your experience and then objectively re-evaluating the situation. Negative reactions and attitudes not only degrade your experience of life, they also influence other people's lives.

6. Ask yourself: what attributes must you acquire in order for your particular desires to be fulfilled?
   - Create your own role model in your imagination. What attributes do they have, and do these resonate with you?
   - Meditate on one of your bigger goals, and see what you are missing. What attributes need to be transformed?
   - Visualize yourself with all the attributes required for success.

Beyond Illusions

My journey of writing this book began when an acquaintance passed away after a long illness. The night after she passed on, I had a dream about her where I was mesmerized by her freedom and immense inner beauty. In the dream, she gracefully guided me to follow a path that I knew was an inner journey to grasp my heart's Desire. As I followed her, I saw the bigger picture of life where the only thing that mattered was the inner gem. The veils, judgments, and life's ambiguity all melted away. Everything merged together and the Truth unfolded. The complexity of life unraveled until I had clarity about myself. I felt self-compassion and immense self-love. I was an observer witnessing myself as a separate entity.

That dream made me understand the meaning of life without external assumptions or layers of misunderstandings that the world had previously imposed on me. I realized that there had been so many missed opportunities because of my lack of understanding of the bigger picture, or because they were obscured by the projections of my limiting thoughts onto the world. At the same time, I realized that there could be no regrets about missed opportunities. Since every decision results in either success or a life lesson, every outcome is for our ultimate benefit. What seems like a failure provides a course correction so that I am redirected to the right path with more clarity, new awareness and increased skills. Therefore, no failure is wasted.

Without self-mastery, we project our limiting thoughts, our experiences in life as mentioned before like a movie projected on a blank screen. After a few minutes of watching the film, we forget about the plain white screen and our reality becomes the action within the movie. We do not see the screen until the movie ends.

While we watch the "movie" of our life, we misjudge, we misperceive, we assume and hence we create separateness and otherness. Turn off the projector and think about the movie that you have been projecting onto your life. After staring at the blank screen for a few seconds, close your eyes, go deep within your heart, and then rediscover your true journey. On this journey, the highest, divine outcome is to do the right thing, to love and respect and honor your Self and others, and to live a life of meaning and significance that honors the unique calling within each of us.

After my dream, I promised that I would always remember one thing: "No more missed opportunities."

Are You Looking for the Tracks of the Lion?

There is a beautiful short story of a hunter and the woodsman that depicts our search for what we desire. A man from the city decided that a real man should be a hunter, so he purchased a rifle and went hunting for a lion in the forest. He asked a woodsman if he had seen the paw prints of a lion. The woodsman said, yes, I have seen it, in fact I will show you the lion himself. The hunter, turning pale and fearful for his life, responded, "No, thank you, I am only searching for his tracks—not the actual lion."

This story represents how most of us are really not sure if we are ready for the object of our desires. We are fearful of acquiring what we claim to be seeking, so, even if we ask for guidance, we are not really looking to fulfill our desires. We need to be honest with ourselves. What are we really searching for—the track or the lion? If we are merely looking for the track, what power are we gaining from this search?

The Code

The Basic Concepts of the Develop Unit

The CODE

FELORA ZIARI

Cup of Insight

The endless desire to be right
shapes the story,
masking the truth that hurts;
vibrations heard,
and when heeded,
a journey revealed;

Life is filled with idle fancies,
yours and mine,
against reality;
in ultimate wisdom,
we choose,
not accepting
wisdom has boundaries;

Some desire joy, bliss,
look for the light that hides their shadows;
oblivious of their fragmented mind,
find a passage to satisfy their drunken hearts.

Others, thirsty for the cup of insight,
tear asunder the veil that holds them back,
revealing the wisdom of their choices,
accepting that desires
reflect the state of mind.

The Code

FELORA ZIARI

UNIT 6
EXECUTE

The Code

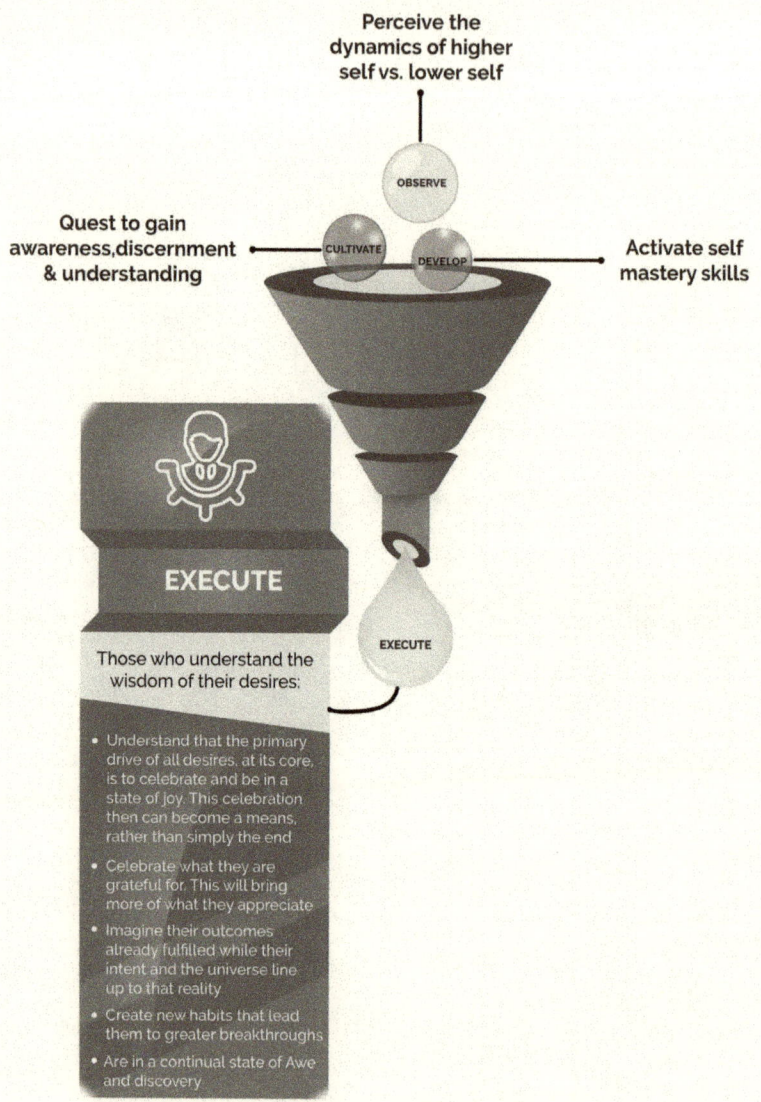

CHAPTER 18
TRANSFORMATION

Some men and women glory in their exalted thoughts, but if these thoughts never reach the plane of action, they remain useless; the power of thought is dependent on its manifestation in deeds.[11]

Breakthroughs

Most of us gain great wisdom and are awakened when we encounter tragedy or heartbreaks. In a way, we are yanked roughly from what we always knew to be true, and are forced to reassess ourselves; to evaluate our lives with the aim of gaining a deeper understanding of who we are and what is important to us. Ram Dass wrote a letter to a family who had lost their young daughter, Rachel. His letter was not just about dealing with a loss; rather, it suggests who we can become because of the loss. When I read this letter many years

---
11 `Abdu'l-Bahá, *Paris Talks*, Bahá'í Publishing Trust, 1999, pgs 17-18.

THE CODE

ago, it transformed my outlook and how I perceived challenges of life. Over the years, this letter has become a source of great consolation and comfort during difficult times. But most importantly, it has helped me to examine my life and have breakthroughs when I was faced with trials and difficulties.

With challenging tests and tragic events, we are compelled to look within ourselves, to examine our values, our courage and our strength. These unfortunate events can make us either more understanding, compassionate, and kinder human beings or they could make us bitter, angry, and sad. We have to make a decision as to how we handle these challenges. Do we move forward and gain more understanding about ourselves, or do we move backwards and become bitter and unhappy?

This is the letter written by Ram Dass to Rachel's family:

Dear Steve and Anita,

Rachel finished her work on earth, and left the stage in a manner that leaves those of us left behind with a cry of agony in our hearts, as the fragile thread of our faith is dealt with so violently. Is anyone strong enough to stay conscious through such teaching as you are receiving? Probably very few. And even they would only have a whisper of equanimity and peace amidst the screaming trumpets of their rage, grief, horror and desolation.

I can't assuage your pain with any words, nor should I. For your pain is Rachel's legacy to you. Not that she or I would inflict such pain by choice, but there it is. And it must burn its purifying way to completion. For something in you dies when you bear the unbearable, and it is only in that dark night of the soul that you are prepared to see as God sees, and to love as God loves.

Now is the time to let your grief find expression. No false strength. Now is the time to sit quietly and speak to Rachel, and thank her for being with you these few years, and encourage her to go on with whatever her work is, knowing that you will grow in compassion and wisdom from this experience. In my heart, I know that you and she will meet again and again, and recognize the many ways in which you have known each other. And when you meet you will know, in a flash, what now is not given to you to know: Why this had to be the way it was.

Our rational minds can never understand what has happened, but our hearts—if we can keep them open to God—will find their own intuitive way. Rachel came through you to do her work on earth, which includes her manner of death. Now her soul is free, and the love that you can share with her is invulnerable to the winds of changing time and space.

As Ram Dass mentioned in the above letter, tests can purify us, burn the impurities within us until we realize that the only thing we are in control of, is our reaction. It is not how we cope with tragedy or grief but how we can reform and refine ourselves. These challenges are our greatest teachers; through them, we shed our veils and idle fancies and become a torchbearer for truth. Through these hard times, we are able to understand what is really important in life, and what really matters. We are then able to guide others out of the darkness of limitations.

It is possible to learn these valuable life lessons without the pain of tragedies and hardships when we **decide** to live our lives from a place of *Honor, Love, Integrity and Compassion* regardless of external influences and to be detached from vain imaginings, becoming a seeker of truth—but we must decide.

> *It is possible to learn life lessons without the pain of tragedies when we decide to live our lives from a place of Honor, Love, Integrity and Compassion regardless of external influences – detached from vain imaginings as a seeker of truth.*

Conscious living, conscious thoughts, conscious language, and conscious intentions are great tools that support an inspired life using the principles of Honor, Love, Integrity, and Compassion.

FELORA ZIARI

Conscious Language

In Zen, there is a saying that reveals something about the dichotomy of good and bad:

To an unenlightened soul, harmful words are like letters carved in stone. As we progress, the words are written in sand. Still farther along, they are written with a stick in water. Finally, the words are written in the air.

Communication is an essential aspect of our lives. Effective and positive communication can enhance our relationships. Communication starts with a thought. The thought is then transmitted to others through our words, body language and our actions. Each aspect of the process of conveying the thought can influence the outcome.

Conscious language is an aspect of mindfulness. Words can bring tears to someone's eyes, sadden someone's heart, or they can elevate, heal, empower and bring joy to hearts. Words leave impressions in the hearer that can have long-term psychological impact. When we weave consciousness into the method, delivery and content of our communications, we create an enriching experience for all involved. We are at peace and create peace through conscious communication.

To execute our goals and our vision into plans, we need to elevate our communication patterns so that they are aligned with our inspired vision to create the desired outcome. As mentioned in the earlier chapters, everything has an energy and is charged with either high vibrational or low vibrational energy. Our words, just like our thoughts, have energy. If they are charged with positive energy, the result will likely be positive. If they are charged with negative energy, the result will be negative.

> *The difference between the almost right word and the right word is really a large matter. 'tis the difference between the lightning bug and the lightning. —Mark Twain*

Science has proven that positive words have the power to change our brain and promote the brain's cognitive functioning. According to Andrew Newberg, M.D. and Mark Robert Waldman[12], positive words like peace and love push the motivational centers of the brain into action, and build resiliency. Negative words, on the other hand, increase the activity in the fear center of the brain, which shuts down the logic and reasoning centers that are located in the frontal lobes.

> *Kind words evoke kindness in the heart*
> *Compassionate words create hope*
> *Insightful words encourages inspired deeds*

The conscious choice of language not only affects our brain, but also impacts how others perceive us. The following are some examples of powerful positive words that can replace negative, limiting words and elevate the impact of our communication:

- Drop negative words such as: never, nobody, do not, cannot, etc.

---

[12] Newbert, Andrew & Waldman, Mark, *Words Can Change Your Brain: 12 Conversation Strategies to Build Trust, Resolve Conflict, and Increase Intimacy*, Avery, 2013.

- Instead, use positive words like: everybody, I do, I can, I will.
- Drop should, need to, have to, ought to or must from your vocabulary, instead use "I choose to ..."
- Drop "I'll try." Instead use "I will." When you say, "I'll try ...," already you are telling yourself that you are going to fail.
- Drop the word "but." For example "He is a nice person, but ..." Whenever "but" follows a complement, the following remark is almost always negative.

Manly Hall, a Canadian born author and mystic, known for his 1928 work, *The Secret Teachings of All Ages*[13], said, "words work on three levels, those that evoke truth, evoke hope or evoke fear."

By consciously choosing powerful and positive words and a high vibrational tone, we can change our attitude, our influence on the outcome and our experience. We can consciously choose to evoke truth and hope, and positively impact our own attitude as well as those of others.

Conscious Intention

*Intention is at the core of all conscious lives.
Conscious intention colors and moves everything.*
—Master Hsing Yun

---

13 Hall, Manly P., *The Secret Teachings of All Ages*, Tarcher Perigee; 2003.

The Code

Conscious intention can help us live our lives in a state of balance and fulfillment. Consider this story:

Joe has a very high IQ and gets an engineering degree with honors. He wants to make a lot of money, so he adds a law degree and switches from working in global refineries to generating patents for large companies. After working for several firms in several years while complaining that "practicing law is a drag," he tries to go back to engineering but is found to be overqualified. Joe's outlets for his frustration, and the two things he enjoys most, are building things at home and working with 'high-risk' youths in robotic machine competitions for which he wins statewide recognition. Still, over the years of pouring over patent law, schematics, and contracts every day, his outlook on life has become increasingly negative. One day, he is talking with a good friend who has a machine shop and wants it to grow. Joe starts coaching him, with a large part of him wishing he could just take over and do the things he is recommending. Joe blurts out his desire, and then like a cosmic explosion, his friend says, "Let's do this!"

Joe draws a line in the sand of his life. With nothing to lose but a paycheck from his law clients, he quits his practice, puts his house up for sale, packs his belongings, and then moves 200 miles away into a one-bedroom, guest house with his two dogs to begin building a business, and making custom components for the energy industry. The whole process took two weeks.

Now, friends and family hardly recognize him because of his new facial expression. His enthusiasm about everything is contagious. His lifelong passion of building things has turned into his livelihood. His work is now his joy, and vice versa.

The practice of conscious intention creates miraculous results in our daily lives. We become more focused and attuned to what we want to create in our lives.

By setting conscious intentions, our interactions, our career, our relationships, and our day in general will greatly improve. When we set intentions, let's say at the beginning of a meeting, we automatically change our mindset to look for opportunities that align with the outcome we have envisioned. We eliminate anything that runs counter to the intentions we have set. We don't waste time, or drain our energy on things that are not aligned with the intentions and the goals we have set.

The Code

CHAPTER 19
THE BIRTH OF A NEW LIFE

What am I looking forward to?

To create an actionable plan, we need to ask the right questions. A great thought-provoking question can stimulate us to conduct a deep inquiry into our lives and move us closer to our inspired goals.

Ask yourself: *What am I looking forward to?* What meaningful and profound milestone must be passed in order to live your life fully and be able to follow your bliss?

Bring back your own curiosity and identify your calling through the following assignment:

> *Get a sheet of paper and scribble down everything that comes to mind regarding the creative urges you have previously squashed, including artistic, expressive, mechanical, conceptual, physical, or anything else you can think of. This can be a list, a mind-map, or a doodle. Stay in the positive, as*

though these things are still possible. Meditate on the words that come to mind, and then take three actions toward following your natural curiosity.

What can you do to look forward to a meaningful life?

- Conscious intention is one of the most powerful tools that can enhance your energy level.
- Everything starts with a thought. Pay attention and consciously choose what you think about. Do not let negative thoughts or a cynical attitude linger or gain power. Briefly examine the impulse that created any negative thoughts then let it pass through you.
- Be aware of the energy produced or created by your behavior or action.
- Embrace both grief and suffering with tenderness. They are experiences that give you insight and understanding of who you are and what you need to learn. Let your heartbreaks become breakthroughs by being open to learn. At the same time, practice self-love and self-compassion by acknowledging the pain you are experiencing and allow it to pass through.

There will always be a struggle between our spiritual world and our physical nature. In the Bahá'í Writings, the spiritual world is described as the real world and the physical world is compared to its shadow.

> *This present life is even as a swelling wave, or a mirage, or drifting shadows. Could ever a distorted image on the desert serve as refreshing waters? No, by the Lord of Lords! Never can reality and the mere semblance of reality be one, and wide is the difference between fancy and fact, between truth and the phantom thereof.*[14]

As you struggle with the duality between the delusion of the physical world and the inner knowing that comes from the spiritual world, you come to understand the limitations of your physical perceptions. You will increasingly trust your spiritual senses to understand the events of your life. You will find that you have great capacity and potential that can be actualized when you face this duality with *self-love* and *self-compassion*. You are able to look forward to fulfilling your desires and following your natural curiosity.

> **Understand the limitations of your physical perceptions.**

Purposeful Commitment

This step demands that you believe that what you desire is not only a wish; it is bigger than you—it is your calling. Ignoring the fears that come and go, and even though you aren't sure how things will work out, you know that you need to do this! Making a commitment requires believing in the worthiness of

---

14 'Abdu'l-Bahá, *Selections From the Writings of 'Abdu'l-Bahá,* Baha'i PublishingTrust, p. 177.

your goal and your power to achieve it without being attached to the precise manifestation of the result. You understand that the universe might have a plan for you that is better than the one with which you started.

> *Life is what happens while you are busy making other plans.* — *John Lennon*

With your inspired goals in mind, you devise a plan that includes your environment, your daily and weekly activities, any requirements to improve your capabilities or skills, your need for service, and your desire to be holistic. Keeping all these commitments requires an unwavering level of will power, which is fortunately one of the differentiators that make us successful and effective human beings.

Ensure that your inspired ideas are rooted in pure thoughts that are free from the shadow side of your ego. Never allow your old assumptions to discredit your newly inspired ideas. They must be acted on. If you fail to act, you will be denying yourself. You will find that you are misaligned with your calling, and then become dissatisfied. Something begins to feel wrong, or someone else starts to look wrong. Pretty soon, you feel that you only have a hammer and everything looks like a nail.

Over time, if you can maintain your commitment, you will create and maintain a spiritual ecosystem in which your passions will thrive. You might create a business project and be driven by the exciting business game. You might start a community, small or large, of people with like-minded passions and pursue a goal together. Notice here that most of these ecosystems exist in relation to other people through rules or agreements. This is how an ecosystem stabilizes.

Planting the seeds of a goal looks like this: Act as if your goal has already been realized successfully. I once heard a leadership coach say, if it is not in the calendar, it does not exist. This includes your friendships; if you do not schedule time to connect, you are unlikely to connect. If you do not make an agreement or give your word to do something outside of your comfort zone, you might find it more difficult to do it when the time comes.

The following statistics were compiled by ASTD (American Society of Training And Development). It shows that the probability of completing a project or goal increases when we have an accountability partner.

- 10% if you hear an idea
- 25% if you consciously decide to adapt it
- 40% if you decide when you will adapt it
- 50% if you have a plan for how you will do it
- 65% if you commit to someone else you will do it
- 95% if you have a specific accountability appointment with the person to whom you committed.

Here is what commitment is not:

- Allowing excuses and circumstances to get in the way of the manifestation of our desires. Where there is a will, there is a way.
- Caving in to previous habits that distract us from achieving the vision we have created.
- Allowing our thoughts and activities to be controlled by the story that was shaped about us by our relatives, teachers, ex-partners, or even by us.

Learn what it means to "choose to choose" something. The nature of true commitment is very active and participative. It gets on the calendar.

Commitment Exercise

Imagine all the commitments to which you are currently obligated. Which ones do you actively choose to choose? Those are your valid commitments. Write them down. Then choose to choose your commitments again—and then again upon waking in the morning, and so on.

What are your commitments to your new vision? Who is your accountability partner?

Success habits

Have you ever wondered why some people are more successful than others? I bet we all have. What is it that they are doing that others are not doing? We can be sure that successful people pay attention to their habits and make sure their habits contribute to superior results. They are more focused, determined and know how to eliminate all the things that are non-essential.

One of the wealthiest men in the twentieth century was Andrew Carnegie. He asked the journalist Napoleon Hill to share his strategies in the bestselling book, *Think and Grow Rich*[15]. In this book, Napoleon Hill emphasized that people that are very successful are very intentional with their habits. They definitely know their purpose and are self-reliant.

In order to create new positive habits, we need to evaluate our old patterns and eliminate the ones that are energy drains or not productive. When our daily routines and habits are aligned with our goals, life flows much more smoothly because we are in balance and in harmony. The following strategies will help you identify and create new habits:

1. Identify the habits that are not producing the outcome you are looking for.

2. Identify the situations that trigger the current habits. Ask yourself what is happening? What are you doing?

3. Identify the reward of each habit. What are you getting from repeating the old habits that are not beneficial anymore?

4. Find another, more positive, habit that can give you the result you are looking for.

---

[15] Hill, Napoleon, *Think and Grow Rich*, CreateSpace Independent Publishing Platform, 2015.

Here are a few habits that you can adopt as part of your daily routine that can enhance your outcome:

- Be intentional about your day, setting specific intentions. Plan your day in advance, either in the morning or the evening before.
- Wake up early.
- Be present to the experiences of life by creating balance in all aspects of life. Quiet your mind chatter through meditation and mantras.
- Be vigilant for positive invitations that life presents to you. Take action on them.
- Incorporate physical exercise into your routine.
- Do not get distracted by every shiny new penny, keep your eyes on the ball and finish the tasks that you identified for the day.
- Eat a healthy diet.
- Take time for *you*.
- Be proactive and not reactive.

CHAPTER 20
ALIGNMENT

Intention of a Successful Restaurateur

We all have the capacity to fulfill our desires by setting an intention and then living our lives as though we had already achieved our goal. As mentioned before, we can create the lives we are looking for by aligning our thoughts, our behaviors and our actions with one cohesive way of life.

> One evening during a recent trip to London, I was dining at a high-end restaurant where I met the restaurant manager, a young flamboyant man, Peter. Peter and I got to know each other through a mutual friend. We talked at length about our life journey and our common fascination with spirituality and how we manifest what we desire in life. He was in the process of opening his own gourmet restaurant. He said he was really excited "to finally realize his dream of opening his own restaurant." Then he told me about his life's

journey and how he came to be where he is.

Peter grew up in a small city in England. Peter and his sister grew up in a single parent household with their mother. They lived a very difficult and challenging life. His mother was a waitress at a local restaurant and was the only one providing for the family.

When he was around 20, with no job, and no prospects, he decided to move to London. Not knowing where he should go, he decided if his main desire was to be successful then he needed to be surrounded by successful people. He said goodbye to his family and took the bus straight to Kensington where he thought accomplished and successful people live.

With his bag in his hand, he stopped at one of the better hotels to ask if they had a job opening. They said they had an opening for a server. They asked him whether he had previous experience in a restaurant? He said, "Of course." even though he had never worked in that field before. He got the job. On his second day, he made many mistakes serving. His superior called him to his office and told him that it was evident that he did not have any experience serving in restaurants. He told his supervisor that it might appear that he had been dishonest, but in his mind, he did not lie. He told him that even though he might not have done the job before, in his mind he had always envisioned that one day he would own his own restaurant and that he had a great desire and passion to be in this industry. Impressed with his straightforwardness and his conviction, the supervisor trained him to be a server.

Twenty years later, his dream of opening a high-end restaurant and being accepted by high society was coming true.

If Peter had not had the desire for success and the courage to take action, he would not have manifested the outcome he had always envisioned. He imagined who he wanted to be and acted accordingly from the beginning.

> *We can create the life we are looking for by aligning our thoughts, our behaviors and our actions with one cohesive way of life.*

Imagining New Possibilities

Desire is our heart's creative power; one that allows the unfolding of our highest truth. It takes the form of passion, which causes the transmutation of the energy of our 'inner knowing' into its destined creative outcome.

Allowing yourself to generate a vision of a life that you would absolutely love, and then letting go of any familiar but obsolete visions, creates new adventures beyond your expectations. That is when you lovingly and enthusiastically challenge yourself and create excitement.

Somewhere in your soul, your wisdom and your passion have produced a blueprint for success that cries out to be unrolled, visualized and manifested. If you fuel your desire with a clear vision, the object of desire becomes your primary goal. When that vision lights you up, you will experience passion and time accelerating.

When true humility exists, we realize that we all have limitations, but we don't have to sulk over that; we can invite Grace into our lives so that our outlook and actions are not based on our own limitations or the limitations of others but on the Grace that emanates from a higher Source. That Grace will help us to discern the truth if we suspend judgment, open our hearts and avoid conclusions based on acquired prejudices or on the ego structures that got developed early in our lives.

Creativity, imagination and inspiration are the outcomes of the wisdom we gain when we examine or investigate our lives without preconceived judgments. Judgments and self-limiting beliefs are the root causes of many failures. They make the perception of our life smaller with fewer options, create fear, and keep us from achieving our true potential. *What if we accepted what is in front of us as neither good nor bad? What if, instead of good and bad, we redefined it in terms of what we understand and what we do not understand?* By switching from the black and white thinking of prejudice to the challenge of understanding something unfamiliar, we become more curious; and we are able to be more creative in implementing our plans and achieving our goals.

One day a farmer's only horse ran away. His neighbor came over and said, "I'm so sorry about your horse." Then the farmer said, "Who knows what's good or bad?" The neighbor was confused because this was clearly terrible. The horse was the most valuable thing his friend owned.

But the horse came back the next day, and brought 12 feral horses with him. The neighbor came over to celebrate, "Congratulations on your great fortune!" And the farmer replied again, "Who knows what's good or bad?"

The next day the farmer's son was taming one of the wild horses when he was thrown and broke his leg. The neighbor said, "I'm so sorry about your son." The farmer repeated, "Who knows what's good or bad?"

Sure enough, the next day the army came through the village to recruit healthy young men to go fight in a war, but the son was spared because of his broken leg.

At times, having an attitude of non-judgment opens our eyes, where we can see the world differently and hence react wisely.

You do not have to know the long-term vision of how you will get your desires fulfilled; you only need to imagine a coherent, and heart-aligned version of your future self, enjoying things that you enjoy. Use the following visualization exercise to recapture the essence of your desire:

Visualization Practice

What is the Vision of Life you desire? Write down at least five visions using the following exercise:

- Close your eyes then create a high definition outcome in your imagination.

- Feel how grateful you are now that you have achieved it. Disregard any worries about how you achieved your vision—only imagine the outcome, the state of being and the feelings you experience.

- Imagine what is new, and what has changed. Your new, high-definition outcome now radiates from your heart to those around you. Others will believe it, both far and wide, although your casual acquaintances might recognize it more clearly than your old friends who have preconceived ideas of who you are and of what you are capable.

- Open your eyes and write down the vision

- You can now begin to generate conversations with your clear outcome in mind, even if you choose to keep your ultimate vision private in the beginning. Before it takes root, carefully choose the friends with whom you share your vision. You want to avoid conversations that will question your ability to achieve your goals.

- Take steps in the direction of your desire and the path will reveal itself. Do not worry about how things will happen. You will face your future decisions, and even roadblocks, with clarity of purpose.

- Follow your curiosity.
- Pay attention at all times. Your new conversations, activities, and relationships should always be aligned with your new goals in mind.
  - What conversations am I choosing to engage in?
  - What activities am I choosing to participate in?
  - What relationships am I choosing to get involve in?

From Awareness to Execution

As mentioned before, we are multidimensional beings, and as such, there are many layers to each of us. In the previous chapters, we examined different aspects of our psyche. We talked about awareness as the first step towards creating clarity and unveiling the inner desires.

Awareness is not only about knowledge; rather it is having the ability to reflect on what we know in order to take the *actions* needed to transform our lives. There are many people who don't know how to handle challenges, so they make wrong choices and decisions. When someone points out to them what the problem might be, or how they might resolve the issues, they say, "I know that, but I don't know why I didn't apply it." We are fooling ourselves when we think knowing a beautiful quote or having the knowledge of the concept makes our lives better. It doesn't matter what we know, if we do not implement the knowledge in our lives. Awareness of concepts and taking action are two different things. We need to transform our learning into action.

How can you move beyond awareness and infuse your knowledge into all the activities of your daily life? The following activities can help you apply your knowing into practical actions until they become habits and part of your daily life:

1. Examine Need vs. Want. Observe what you want vs. what you really need. After a while you will realize that most of the things you are seeking come from your "Wants," and not your "Needs." This knowing will help you relax and enjoy life more.

2. Every day, create a "To Do List" outlining everything you can do that day that can get you closer to your inspired goals.

3. You also need to create a "Not To Do List" in addition to your "To Do List." The "Not To Do List" is very important since it will help you eliminate the distractions that can easily hinder your progress.

4. Set at least three intentions every day. Intentions should be positive, practical and based on the "Future Vision" of your goals.

5. Be adaptable and flexible while implementing your vision. When you are too rigid, you stifle the creativity that could inspire you to go beyond what you have planned. Be ready to create something even bigger and better. Remember Bruce Lee's approach to life: Be like Water. It sure helps!

6. Elevate each conversation to a "Future Vision" of where you want to be. Create new opportunities by being open to possibilities of the future vision. Always "see the end at the beginning."

7. Evaluate your motives. When taking actions, ask yourself: What is my motive? Purity of motive will help you attract others who have the same attitude.

8. Pay attention to your habits. Eliminate habits that are not producing good results and create new "Success" habits that allow new learnings to flow into your actions.

9. Remember your unique blueprint, your specific desires through daily reflection and meditation.

10. Silence your chattering mind through meditation by allowing the chatter to pass through without giving it weight. Observe and then let it go. You will not be able to hear your inner calling when distracted by negative lingering thoughts.

11. Eliminate distraction by remembering your three intentions and your "Future Vision."

12. Remember "Time" can be very restrictive. Don't take hasty decisions or compromise your values because you think time is running out. You will create other problems and challenges that could throw you out of balance.

13. There are certain things that you do not know about yourself that can help you with furthering your awareness. These questions can help you understand yourself better and learn what skills you need in order to be a better version of yourself. Ask yourself these "I" questions:

    a) What is it that I know about myself that everyone else knows?

    b) What is it that I know about myself, but no one else knows about me? What am I hiding? Why am I hiding these aspects of myself?

    c) What can I learn from these masks in order to heal or overcome what I am hiding?

    d) What is it that others know about me, that I don't know about myself? Inquire from others. Most of the time other people have a different perception of us than we have about ourselves. When we make inquiries, we learn how we are being perceived. We can learn to find solutions to those aspects of us that are perceived differently than our actual or desired aspects.

e) How can I learn more about my hidden potential and talents? This is where new possibilities can emerge. By being open to explore and asking the right questions, we can learn to develop our hidden potential.

The Code

The basic concepts of the Execute unit.

The Code

FELORA ZIARI

Remember to Remember

A beacon of light,
purpose and hope
when you remember
to Remember!
what has passed!
what was given!
the Truth of what is!
And commitment to Certitude!

In a life full of surprises
full of adventures,
you are given a chance
to be all that you are meant to be!
To remember
the Gift of Love!
the Breath of Life!
the Song of your Soul!

To honor
what has passed!
what was given!
the Truth of what is!
and your commitment
to be all that you are meant to Be!

The Code

FELORA ZIARI

UNIT 7
THE GIFT OF CODE

The Code

CHAPTER 21
BECOMING AN INNER EXPLORER

As a young adult, I always felt as though I was chasing life. I continuously wanted more out of life. I was trying too hard to prove my worth to myself and consequently to others. I was never in the moment, satisfied with what was in front of me. I felt as though I was always frantically searching for *something new*, or *something more*, not really knowing what that something was. Until one day, as if a voice was crying out, I heard myself saying out loud:

> *You KNOW!*

> Did I? Really?

That's when I became an inner-explorer. I say inner-explorer because somewhere, hidden inside all of us, is a kind of Knowing that has been suppressed or ignored. I knew I had to explore my inner knowing in order to find the missing links and achieve the object of my desire ... contentment.

The CODE

I started examining the source of my anguish and discontent. It wasn't easy. I started on a journey of self-discovery and had many moments of insight and deep realization about myself and about life. It took a long time to understand why in the face of my victories, I was still unsatisfied. Those insights were the impetus for writing The CODE.

The most magical wisdom I discovered was that we grow up having many layers of assumptions about ourselves. We don't realize, until we start the journey of inner exploration, that most of these assumptions are actually rooted in the expectations of other people. The story we then told ourselves is that our worth is based on what other people think of us. The other layers of assumptions are based on cultural beliefs, our families' education, fears, and shortcomings. On top of all the assumptions we have absorbed from others are experiences of disappointments, setbacks, and challenges that we have endured. We won't be able to distinguish between truth and assumptions unless we reflect on our total life experiences and explore how different our mindset and our life would have been without those assumptions and expectations. Through deep reflection, we realize that we have covered our assumptions with other assumptions, and then covered them again with whatever hindrances we faced. If we don't learn to uncover what doesn't work and think outside the box of conformity, then, sadly, we would not be able to shift our mindset to learn to expand our way of thinking and reveal our true purpose. That's when we feel trapped in lives of dissatisfaction and continuous search for something more.

The other important aspect of my inner exploration was the lack of understanding of self-love and self-compassion. I realized that most of us do not know how to love ourselves fully. We feel selfish for loving ourselves. However, without having affection and compassion for ourselves, there is no way that we would have complete affection and love for others or be totally present to life. Without self-love, our love for others would be conditional. It would be based on what we need in return and how they can serve us in the future.

Self-love requires courage—courage to abandon self-judgments, and to love each aspect of ourselves for all it has accomplished. Even more importantly, it requires us to love the effort we put into developing all the different traits and qualities that are a "work in progress" and have not yet been fully developed.

However, I realized that in order not to have anxiety and resistance on this journey, I had to rely on two things: trust and detachment. Without these two foundational pillars, it would have been very hard and probably impossible to sustain the momentum and achieve optimization. I realized that in order to pursue my dreams, I had to trust my abilities, and not second-guess myself. I also had to trust the Universe since ultimately I was not in control of what life offers or takes away. Maintaining that trust required that I be detached from the expectation that everything should unfold the way I have planned.

To achieve an outcome that is aligned with our inner desires, we have to make a commitment to ourselves to always "Remember" our values, desires, our uniqueness, and to "see the end at the beginning."

We need to build a new foundation that is stronger than what was handed down to us. That is the secret to experiencing a fulfilling life—to discover who we could be without the limitations of our past, to reveal what holds us in fear and anxiety so we can discard what doesn't work, and learn new things based on our own personal exploration and investigation. That's the gift of CODE!

No matter how deeply we have buried our desires, they are ultimately a force of evolution and growth that cannot be denied. We are here to fulfill a unique purpose in the world, and our desires are clues that lead us directly to the doorsteps of the expression of our destinies. As we live our purpose using the two pillars of Detachment and Trust, our lives will undergo transformation in ways we never thought possible.

Thank you for reading this book.

Felora Ziari

January, 2018

About the Author

Felora Ziari was born in Iran. At seventeen she left Iran and moved to England to pursue an engineering degree at Oxford. She then embarked upon a sixteen-year career as an electro-mechanical engineer and engineering manager in the nuclear industry in the US. She left the private sector to dedicate her time to community service in the non-profit world that included her work in women empowerment, peace building, leadership development and more.

Her passion for transformative action in women led her to establish and manage a non-profit platform for the empowerment of women and girls for 19 years. In the past few years, she founded Crimson Woman and Crimson Global Academy, a leadership and human potential accelerator for women. Through her leadership programs, seminars, workshops, and motivational speeches, women around the world achieved greater success in all aspects of their lives.

She is a founding member of a global non-profit organization called Peace Through Commerce Inc.® (PTC) for which she developed curriculum and led domestic and international training, striving for sustainable peace through entrepreneurial development, and leadership.

Above and beyond her work in the nonprofit sector, Ziari is also a successful business leader, an entrepreneur and a poet. Her book of poetry, *Whispers from Above*, was published in 2014.

Ziari won a humanitarian award for her global philanthropic work in 2012. She believes in the importance of giving back as a means of achieving global peace. To that end, She serves on the board of advisors for the Center for Global Business at McCombs School of Business at University of Texas at Austin. She also serves as the president of the board of the United Nations Association, Austin chapter and has served as the board chair of the Interfaith Action of Central Texas (iACT), and PTC.

Today she resides in Austin, Texas. She is a speaker and a consultant for cultivating leadership and maximizing human potential.

She can be reached through www.felora.net.

www.ingramcontent.com/pod-product-compliance
Lightning Source LLC
Chambersburg PA
CBHW032104090426
42743CB00007B/231